ADHD

How to Promote Better Behavior and Enhance
Academic and Social Skills

(A Guide for Parents and Teens to Help You Gain
Motivation and Confidence)

Jarvis Carter

Published by Rob Miles

© **Jarvis Carter**

All Rights Reserved

Adhd: How to Promote Better Behavior and Enhance Academic and Social Skills (A Guide for Parents and Teens to Help You Gain Motivation and Confidence)

ISBN 978-1-990084-16-4

Legal & Disclaimer

The information contained in this book is not designed to replace or take the place of any form of medicine or professional medical advice. The information in this book has been provided for educational and entertainment purposes only.

The information contained in this book has been compiled from sources deemed reliable, and it is accurate to the best of the Author's knowledge; however, the Author cannot guarantee its accuracy and validity and cannot be held liable for any errors or omissions. Changes are periodically made to this book. You must consult your doctor or get professional medical advice before using any of the suggested remedies, techniques, or information in this book.

Table of Contents

Introduction

Underᴛtanding of ADHD in Children And Adultᴛ: The brain communicateᴛ messages through neuronᴛ in the brain. But at the end of every neuron there iᴛ a gap called a synapse. The

meᴛᴛage needᴛ to jump between the gapᴛ, and doeᴛ thiᴛ with the aid of a chemical called a neurotranᴛmitter produced by the

body. "Perᴛonᴛ with ADHD tend not to releaᴛe enough of theᴛe

eᴛᴛential chemicalᴛ, or to releaᴛe and reload them too quickly

before an adequate connection has been made." In effect, meᴛᴛ ageᴛ ᴛtruggle to get where they need to go to be acted on.

Medications, including ᴛtimulantᴛ and non-ᴛtimulantᴛ, help

make up for theᴛe deficitᴛ by triggering the releaᴛe of certain chemicals, which in turn

1

help the neuronт to communicate with each other.

Currently, the Diagnoттic and Statiттical Manual (DSM-IV) of Mental Health Disorders—the handbook uтed by mental health profeттionalт to аттетт and diagnoтe ADHD—does not include тupporting information on the link between ADHD and emotion regulation.

Finally, it'т important to highlight that while a perтon with ADHD will тtruggle with a variety of тymptomт that fall under inattention and/or impulтivity and hyperactivity, in almoтt every

caтe there will be areaт where the person is able to focus intently, тometimeт referred to aт "hyper-focuт." This is typically тeen in areas that the person тhowт a great intereтt in, тuch aт playing video gameт, playing a muтical inттrument or even reading when the тubject matter haт great appeal.

4 If you or тomeone you love suffers from ADHD (Attention Deficit/Hyperactivity Diтorder), you've probably spent what

feels like a lifetime searching for a treatment that reduces the

τymptomτ without all the negative τide effectτ. Now, you can τtop looking. CBD oil might be juτt the τolution you've been hoping for. If you're curious about uτing CBD oil for ADHD, you've come to the right place.

Attention-Deficit

Hyperactivity

Diτorder

(ADHD)

is

aneurodevelopmental condition that affectτ both children and adultτ.

Almoτt eleven percent of American children have ADHD. But it's not just a childhood diτorder. About four percent of American adults have ADHD aτ well. It is thought to be genetic, with some environmental factorτ playing a role aτ well. ADHD is more prevalent in children living in lower-income households, which тuggeтtт that environment iт indeed тignificant.

There is a long tradition of people with ADHD using CBD and other cannabis productт to treat their condition. While it may тeem counterintuitive to some, this iт mainly because of the

pтychoactive propertieт aттociated with the THC in cannabiт.

The non-psychoactive CBD, however, haт shown reтultт in managing ADHD.

While there iт not a ton of research into CBD oil aт a treatment for ADHD, the тtudieт done thus far have been promiтing. Since

CBD alтo haт the effects of improving mood and decreaтing anxiety, which are often preтent in sufferers of ADHD, it iт likely

to have poтitive reтultт even if it doeт not affect the underlying diтorder.

5 More research is neceттary to determine whether CBD will become a mainттream

treatment for ADHD. Controlled studies тhould be conducted in the near future, due to the medical field'т current intereтt in CBD, as well aт increaтing legality

making such studies possible.

Chapter 1: Infancy – Toddler Years

No matter how much we try to structure our lives and be in control of everything that happens to us, events will occur that we did not anticipate or imagine and will serve as tests to our strength and character as a person. My son was born on the 8th day of the blistering hot month of July in the year 1999. The nurses pronounced him to be a healthy baby boy at 7lbs and 8ounces. He was my first child, so like every new mother I doted on his every move, crawl, coo, and smile. His father and I named him Gerard Garrison Hearst. My career had been my focus during my early twenties and I delayed pregnancy until I was well advanced in my career and in age – much to my family's chagrin. I was 28 when I gave birth to him and my family members breathed a sigh of relief when it happened. Gerard's father had been my boyfriend since the age of 16 and we were engaged at the time of his birth. We were high school and college sweethearts; however our relationship did not last. Our ideas about relationships and commitment were not aligned. We decided to part ways and still remain the best parents that we could be for our son.

Despite the rocky start to motherhood I was extremely happy to be a new mom and embraced the challenge with a huge smile on my face. Gerard slept well when I brought him home from the hospital and was a sweet baby that I enjoyed spending my day with when I was not working. I decided to stay home with him until he turned 18 months, at which time I enrolled in graduate school. I placed him in day care and his paternal grandmother would keep him during the week too. He was a joy to watch as he was all boy; running, jumping, falling, and constantly on the go. Gerard would run around with all of his cousins, ignoring all my yelling, and play well with his friends. He also napped at least two hours during the day and slept well at night.

As a toddler, Gerard was a joy to be around and watch grow. He was not a temperamental child. Even though I was a first time mother, he did not create a challenge that I could not fix or soothe which had me feeling like an award winning mother. When he was one year old, I was a personal trainer in her late twenties, so I had a great amount of energy. I placed him in the Apple Tree Academy daycare when he turned 20 months old. He really enjoyed going to school and I never noticed that he was a busy child because, well, the plan was to keep him busy throughout the day. We took daily park trips in the neighborhood as well as daily trips downtown to feed the birds. I loved the outdoors (and since Gerard came out of me I assumed he would too), so I bought a bike and took him on adventurous trails of nature. Boy was I right about him, Gerard and I would go to the bike trail and ride for hours so that he could see nature and feel the Georgia breeze on his face. You could see from his smiles how much he loved those trips. He would often fall asleep on the way home from our bike rides. He was a playful toddler who loved Blues Clues simply because he loved to draw and write in his "handy dandy" notebook. He could hold a conversation with literally everyone that he met. He never met a stranger that he did not like or approach to speak to. People often commented to me that his personality and attitude was the nicest that they had seen since the early eighties when children were respectful. I would tell them that he was born like that; I never had to teach him to be respectful - God made him that way and I loved it. His manners were admired by me, family members, and others that he met.

As Gerard grew older, he became more active, but nothing that I could not handle. I noticed that he had a huge amount of energy when we would arrive home in the afternoon. At night he sometimes had a hard time going to sleep at his bedtime. I knew that it was important to fill his days with more activities to ensure that he was tired by nightfall so he could get the amount of sleep needed to be productive during the day. In a desperate attempt to give him more play time and wear out his energy, I registered him for the Little Gym twice a week. He played and interacted with children his age and the instructor made sure he kept him busy. My son really loved going there on Tuesday and Thursday afternoons. The Little Gym was the key to having him tired and ready for bed. He had less energy when we arrived home; mission accomplished!

When Gerard was three he advanced to the three year old room in daycare. His teachers Ms. Amanda and Ms. Fushia adored him as he was very sweet to them and the other children in the classroom. They told me that he did not take naps during the two hour nap period but instead he would play with his shoe by tying and untying the laces. Now I had noticed his laces were always tied different than the way I tied them in the morning but I just thought that was funny, picturing him tying and untying his shoes for two hours. His teachers asked me if I could bring coloring books and crayons for him to color during nap time, so I took the crayons and coloring book to school for him to find his inner artist. Gerard may have colored only once in that book during the entire year.

His teachers never complained about him not napping though. I figure that if he remained quiet on his mat, then they were ok with him not taking naps. Happily and hopeful, Gerard graduated to Pre-K thanks to his teachers who were great with him and patient. I was so thankful that there were never any complaints from his teachers about his napping or talking. He seemed to be the teacher's pet. They also did not complain about his ability to climb and jump on objects that boys loved to jump on. These were actions that my son surely exhibited, but I could handle it considering I thought all boys were the same. I was just extremely thankful that he was not defiant, moody, or had conduct and behavioral issues like some children experience.

Chapter 2: Is Adhd A Mental Disorder? A Learning Disorder? Something Else Entirely?

Technically, ADHD is considered a mental disorder. It is also considered a learning disability. The good news is this disorder does not carry the same social stigma that comes with many other mental disorders. There are so many people living with and being diagnosed with this disorder today, that it is very commonplace and raises no eyebrows when it is mentioned. From a social perspective, this is great news for those suffering with ADHD.

From a medical perspective, this might not be such a blessing. Since the disorder is believed to affect so many people, there are some problems that sufferers come up against:

1. Some teachers are quick to diagnose children in their own minds without any testing to prove their theory. They may push parents toward medication or assume the disorder is to blame for all bad behavior displayed in their classroom. ADHD medication is seen as the quick fix for children who do not sit quiet and do as they are told perfectly. This can be dangerous. Please read more about ADHD and the school system in chapter four.

2. Parents sometimes struggle to find doctors willing to take their concerns about ADHD seriously. Some doctors will downplay the symptoms reported by parents, while others are too eager to prescribe medlation without properly evaluating and diagnosing the child. Parents have to jump through hoops to make sure their child is properly diagnosed, since there are other mental disorders that can exhibit many of the same symptoms. As you will discover in the final chapter of this book, sometimes

ADHD will be present along with another mental or learning disorder.

3. Adults are not always taken seriously when they tell medical professionals they want to be tested for ADHD. It is believed that around 60% of ADHD children carry the disorder into adulthood, and many never receive a proper diagnosis. Read chapter eleven to learn more about the disorder as it relates to the work life of adult sufferers. It is very similar to what children go through at school, but your boss is much less likely to recommend treatment than a teacher in elementary school.

4. There is a lot of confusion over the use of medication to treat ADHD. Some are against it, others are scared of it, and still others are too casual in its use. Read chapter seven to understand what medications are typically prescribed and what risks may come with them for adults and children.

On one hand, diagnosing ADHD is very easy and is done every day. On the other hand, it may be so common today that many medical professionals no longer realize how serious it is for the sufferer. It is on the adult sufferer or the parent of a sufferer to seek out professionals who can properly diagnose and treat the disorder.

Chapter 3: Symptoms And Effects Of Adult Add/Adhd

People need to understand that the signs and symptoms of attention deficit disorder vary between children and adults. The symptoms can also greatly vary from one adult to another. Here are just some of the most common symptoms of ADD. You can use this list to have a quick assessment but you will need to consult with a mental health expert to get a more accurate diagnosis.

1. You have difficulty in concentration

Adults suffering from ADD frequently find it difficult to concentrate on even everyday tasks such as cooking or doing the laundry. They can get easily sidetracked by even the slightest change in imagery or noise level. People notice that they can suddenly jump from one endeavor to another or they can easily become uninterested and inattentive. This symptom is often ignored because it is not as disrupting as the other symptoms such as being overly active and always acting on impulse. You can check if you have any of these indications:

* You sometimes zone out without noticing it. You will just hear people You can be extremely distracted during conversations. It is therefore challenging for you to keep tabs on the topic being discussed.

* You struggle to finish any task you started; this goes for both the simple and complicated ones.

* You tend to miss important details so you end up making mistakes and suffering mishaps when you are trying to do your job.

* You find it hard to listen to other people, especially when you are given instructions or directions.

2.You are hyperfocused

Almost everyone is aware that individuals suffering from ADD often find it difficult to focus on a job that does not interest them. What people are not aware of is that the exact opposite is also a symptom of ADD. Hyperfocus is the propensity to be fully engrossed in activities that are exciting and satisfying.

If you think about it, a person with ADD uses hyperfocus as a means to cope with poor concentration. Through hyperfocus, he or she can tune out all the distractions that keep him or her from focusing. In some cases, hyperfocus can become so intense that a person can become highly unaware of everything else that is happening around him or her.For instance, you may become too absorbed reading an interesting novel or watching a television program that you completely forget to do the other chores that need to be done. Hyperfocus can be a good thing when used to channel a person's attention towards creative and constructive endeavors, but if it is left unrestrained, it can result in trouble in both professional and personal relationships.

3.You are disorganized and forgetful

If you are suffering from ADD, you will feel that your day-to-day life appears to be filled with chaos and problem after problem. You can try to organize your schedule and your surroundings but they always end up disorganized at the end of the day. You find it hard to sort out the things that you need for completing the tasks that are assigned to you. Your priorities are all scrambled that people often go to you to remind you about missed deadlines or incomplete tasks. Here are some of the other indications of being disorganized and forgetful:

* You have inadequate organizational abilltles. Your house, your workstation at the office, and even your car can almost always be found as untidy and disorderly.

* You tend to give in to procrastination.

* You have difficulty beginning and completing tasks.

* You are always late for work and appointments.

* You always forget scheduled meetings and important dates.

* You always misplace your personal stuff like keys and your phone.

* You tend to underestimate the required time for finishing your activities.

4.You are highly impulsive

If you are suffering from this symptom, you probably always catch yourself saying remarks and replies that you don't really want to say out loud. You hear people telling you that you act before you think. You may respond too quickly to other people's actions and words without trying to understand what they truly mean. Because you are impulsive, you tend to become very impatient when you need to sit still and wait. This symptom can actually bring you risks or danger becayse you hastily do things without thinking about the consequences first. Here are some of the other indications of being impulsive:

* You butt in during conversations and you do not wait for other people to finish what they are saying before you speak.

* You lack self-control.

* You tend to utter offensive or improper remarks because you do not think before you speak.

* You have a higher tendency to be addicted to nicotine, caffeine, alcohol, and other substances.

* You find it hard to behave appropriately during social gatherings.

5.You find it hard to control your emotions

Adults who suffer from ADD often find it difficult to handle emotions, especially the strong emotions like rage and annoyance. If you have any of the following indications, you may be suffering from ADD:

* You often feel that you are an underachiever.

* You find it hard to control your feelings when you are frustrated at something.

* You can easily become irritated and your mood can easily change from good to bad.

* You find it difficult to sustain your motivations.

* You are very sensitive to the criticisms given by other people.

* You can easily lose your temper and you can get very angry even for the most irrelevant thing.

* You suffer from low self-confidence and you often feel insecure.

6.You are often hyperactive or restless

Hyperactive adults suffering from ADD basically act similarly to hyperactive children who also suffer from the disorder. You feel like you are always full of energy and you want to continuously move around to release your extra energy. However, this hyperactivity tendency can become more restrained as persons with ADD become older because the hyperactivity tends to stay inside the head instead of being expressed externally.

Here are some of the other indications of being hyperactive or restless:

* You feel agitated internally. Even if you try to meditate, you cannot calm down your mind because various thoughts keep barging into your head.

* You often take risks that can jeopardize your life, relationships, or even finances.

* You often find yourself fighting with boredom.

* You can never really sit still. When you are sitting or waiting in line, you often find yourself squirming, twitching, or fiddling.

* You always crave for exciting activities.

* You tend to talk in excess and people need to ask you to quiet down sometimes.

* You like to do several tasks all at the same time.

Various Effects of Adult ADD

Most probably, you are reading this book because you believe that you are suffering from attention deficit disorder. You may have endured some mean labels from other people who call you "slothful/lazy" or "slow/stupid."Deep inside, you know that you can do better in life but the symptoms discussed above seem to always hinder you from being the person you want to become. And because you cannot control yourself, you start to believe all those negative labels that other people give you. If you ignore the symptoms above and decide not to undergo proper diagnosis and treatment, you may suffer from the following problems for the rest of your life:

Physical and Mental Health

* You may become overweight because you cannot control the amount of food that you eat.

* You may become an alcoholic or a drug addict because you may be too weak to control yourself against these harmful substances.

* You may suffer from depression or anxiety because of the persistent pressure and stress that you experience in your daily life.

* You may suffer from other diseases that remain undiagnosed because you keep forgetting your appointment with your physician.

* Your existing diseases may not be properly treated because you also forget to drink your medicines at the proper times.

Career and Finance

* You may find it difficult to hold a job so you keep resigning and looking for a new one.

* You can also get into trouble at work because you find it hard to adhere to the rules and regulations of your company.

* You may become frustrated because you don't get promoted. Your boss may often complain about your late deliveries or submissions and persistent tardiness.

* You incur additional charges and fees because you forget to pay your bills on time.

* You may find yourself deep in debt because you cannot control your spending.

Relationships

* Your relationship with your spouse or partner may be strained because you are getting tired of his or her endlessly nagging you about your behavior.

* Your family may find it difficult to live with you because you are messy and disorganized.

* Your spouse or partner may think that you don't care for him or her because you don't pay attention to what he or she is saying and you zone out.

* Your family and friends may think you are insensitive when you keep forgetting special occasions.

Chapter 4: 10 Signs Of Adhd

ADHD is a clinical diagnosis. That is, it is based on observations and conversations. Included in these observations is the very important collection of information about your childhood, your parents and other relatives. All these observations are combined with how the person acts in daily life.

There are many different symptoms of ADHD. As different as people are generally, as many different ADHD symptoms exist.

It is possible that you might have ADHD when ...:

You find yourself sorting your children's books in alphabetical order, when you were supposed to be doing the laundry.

When you have ADHD it is enormously difficult to motivate yourself to do daily chores. But at the same time some have a tendency to hyper focus on small unimportant details and often find it enormously difficult to detach themselves.

You are about to explode at the smallest trivialities.

It is often seen in people with ADHD, that they have great difficulty in controlling their temper.

You show up for a meeting at 08:00pm at New Street 6 when in reality you had to have been at New Street 8 at 06.00pm.

People with ADHD often have a lack of sense of time and can often reverse the order of information.

Your child is diagnosed with ADHD.

ADHD may seem to be hereditary. When a family member has it, there is approximately 25% to 35% chance that another person in the family will also have it.

You finally get to bed at two o'clock in the morning, even though you had decided to go to bed at 10 o'clock

When you have ADHD, it can often be difficult to follow a circadian rhythm.

One regularly returns to the bill that should have been paid three months ago.

It can often be difficult to get bills paid and manage money. When you have ADHD, you often lose the big picture.

You are in the process of starting your seventh major project without completing the six previous ones.

It is often difficult to keep your motivation to finish projects. On the other hand, there are many with ADHD who are very creative and have 1000 good ideas and thoughts.

Every time you walk past the television, you will be mesmerized and completely absorbed, and then you discover that you are standing with open mouth and staring at an episode of " Bob the Builder".

When you have ADHD, you have no filter to screen out irrelevant sensations.

You constantly find excuses for why you should not do the washing up.

Many people with ADHD often have great difficulty in meeting deadlines. You are procrastinating constantly. Only when deadlines are being exceeded and you have "a gun to their head", are you able to get some work done.

Nearly every morning, you are running around, shouting and screaming at the family, because you cannot find your keys.

People with ADHD often lose things. When you have to deal with all your sensations at the same time it can be difficult to be aware that you have put your key down. Therefore the brain does not register where you put them, or indeed, that you have put them down.

Chapter 5: History Of Adhd

ADHD also known as Attention Deficit Hyperactivity Disorder, has been around for quite a while. Some believed it was just the child being willful and others blamed poor parenting. Parents blamed it on poor teachers. The fact is, that the cause of ADHD is not understood. Life events such as a death, a divorce, or proceeding can trigger ADHD like behaviors.

In the 1930's physicians set forth the notion that amphetamines alleviate the symptoms of ADHD. They could also reduce impulsivity and hyperactivity as well. They were quite effective.

Stimulants became the standard of treatment for ADHD in the 1950's. They continue to be effective in relieving ADHD. They continued to increase in popularity in the 1960's and it is now believed that ADHD has a physical cause.

The name switched to Attention Deficit Disorder in the beginning of the 1980s from minimal brain disorder. Because of the fact that many children were also demonstrating hyperactive behaviors it was renamed to Attention Deficit Hyperactivity Disorder.

A 12-hour release drug was launched. Around 2001- 2002 some guidelines were set up. A physical check is strongly advised and doctor and the patient should work together for successful treatment. Stimulants were the prescription that is recommended.

The targets made for them by the physician should be met by a kid. Periodic check-ups should be done with appropriate oversight by a medical specialist. Jointly with the FDA doctors in 2002 had introduced a non-stimulant drug. There must be an accurate identification and attention.

The side effects of stimulant drugs are dangerous. They are extremely addictive. Sleeplessness, depression, and a reduced desire have been noticed with just short term use. Kids who take stimulant drugs for a very long time are as adults more likely to have depression and substance abuse issues.

Natural treatments are available such as medications that are made out of herbs together with vitamins and minerals which can be known to help ADHD. They are free from harmful side effects, dyes, and additives (dyes and preservatives). They're not dangerous for use in the long term or the short term. The nutritional supplements should be both FDA approved and made by a professional that is homeopathic certified.

They help to bring a child's head and body into balance and this allows for greater success and better focus. Together with lots of exercise, a good healthy diet, and plenty of sleep the supplements round out things.

In this day and age, you would think that ADHD has been around forever. It was only lately that it was given the name Attention Deficit Disorder, although the illness itself has been around for quite some time. Before that, the illness had various names that transformed over the years.

In 1902, the first official ailment connecting to impulsiveness was recognized. It was in Britain, and the physician who diagnosed the impulsive disorder was named Dr. Still. He called this ailment "Defect of Moral Control" and he considered that the diagnosed person had a medical illness beyond their control.

Next occasion, the next documentation of similar symptoms was in 1922. Here, the symptoms we associate with ADHD were given the name "Post-Encephalitic Behavior Disorder." That was the name during this time period, although what this title means I 'm not quite certain.

The next occasion in the history of ADHD was in 1937, where Dr. Charles Bradley introduced the use of stimulants in children who were hyperactive. I however find it interesting that stimulants were thought of to treat hyperactive children when they were already bouncing off the walls. How did someone hypothesize that this would happen, while it is true that hyperactive children calm down? In 1956, after this, Ritalin was introduced as the drug of choice to treat hyperactivity.

In the 1960s, a broader group of citizens used stimulants. The only symptom which was really recorded at this point was hyperactivity. In the early 1960s, the illness was called "Minimal Brain Dysfunction". At the end of the decade, though, the name of the disorder was changed to "Hyperkinetic Disorder of Youth."

In 1980, the ailment was given its present name of Attention Deficit Disorder, with or without hyperactivity. This was recorded in the DSM III put out by the American Psychiatric Association. ADD and ADHD were two different diagnoses.

Next, in 1987, ADD was shifted to Attention Deficit Hyperactivity Disorder. The American Psychiatric Associated noted that this is a medical diagnosis, and not just psychological. Additionally, they noted that ADHD could cause behavioral issues.

In 1996, a fresh medication called Adderall was approved by the FDA for the treatment of ADHD. After a period of time, it was deemed to be better at treating the ailment since it was simpler to get out of and lasted longer. In 1999, other drugs were added to treat ADHD for example Concerta and Focalin. In 2003, Strattera was introduced as the first ADHD drug that was not a stimulant. This drug worked like an antidepressant, but raised the number of norepinephrine in the brain.

Chapter 6: The 10 Common Myths And Misconceptions About Adhd

There are a number of disorders and psychological conditions that are much debated about and ADHD is one of them. There are many mistaken beliefs, myths and misconceptions surrounding ADHD, its causes and symptoms.

The purpose of this chapter is to take you through the 10 common misconceptions about ADHD and the truth that debunks the myths. Pay special attention to the ones regarding children suffering from ADHD, as there might be certain things that you, as a parent, might have completely misunderstood for long.

Myth 1: Boys are more likely to suffer from ADHD

Fact: Girls are as likely to suffer from ADHD as boys. There is no scientific or genetic reason behind the boys being at a greater risk of getting affected by the condition. However, since this continues to be a popular myth, boys are more likely to be diagnosed with ADHD than girls.

Myth 2: Bad parenting results in ADHD

Fact: Rude behavior, bad language and the hyperactive nature of a child suffering from ADHD cannot be attributed entirely to the lack of good parenting skills. So calm down, it's not you who have not taught your child about how to behave right. Rather, it's because of the inability of your child to control his or her impulse. Strict parenting with such children might even make their behavior worse, thus warranting a need for a professional intervention.

Myth 3: ADHD and other psychiatric disorders cannot co-occur

Fact: The truth is that a person suffering from ADHD is six times more likely to suffer from other psychiatric and learning disorders, in addition to anxiety and depression. A majority of ADHD cases overlaps with other problems.

Myth 4: ADHD is all about having behavioral problems and being hyperactive

Fact: ADHD is a complex disorder, which is not just about having a problem with the behavior and simply not listening to anybody. It is a disorder that involves the brain chemistry, which, in turn, affects and impairs the cognition, memory, organization, emotional modulation and motivation, in addition to the other brain functions.

Myth 5: Children with ADHD eventually outgrow their conditions as they become adults

Fact: It is estimated that more than 70 percent of the children with ADHD continue to suffer from the disorder as they reach adolescence and almost 50 percent of the children continue to have the disorder as adults.

In addition, it is estimated that nearly 6 percent of the adults have ADHD and most of them remain either undiagnosed or do not seek any active treatment. Since responsibilities and workload increases with age, adults with ADHD may find it difficult to organize and complete the tasks. In addition, they are at a greater risk of facing financial, professional, legal and personal problems, as compared to the other normal adults of the same age. The purpose of this information is not to dishearten you, but to prepare you for the upcoming challenges.

Myth 6: People with ADHD are incapable of doing any intellectual work

Fact: This is one of the most common myths associated with ADHD. Children and people with ADHD might seem ignorant, but research conducted in the past has revealed that they actually have above-average intelligence. In fact, such individuals are not even lazy. Many high-achieving and well-known personalities from the past, including Abraham Lincoln, Benjamin Franklin, Mozart and George Bernard Shaw, are thought to have had suffered from the disorder.

Myth 7: ADHD medications put the children at the risk of abusing drugs as an adult

Fact: The fact is actually the other way around. Not providing a proper treatment to a child suffering from ADHD might actually increase the risk of them abusing alcohol or drugs during their adulthood. The drugs that are prescribed to an ADHD patient do not actually cure the disorder. These clinically tested and effective medicines are just used to help reduce the severity of the symptoms.

Myth 8: Only hyperactive kids have ADHD

Fact: While hyperactivity is one of the common symptoms of ADHD, it is not mandatory for a child to show this symptom to be suffering from the condition. Therefore, your child might be suffering from ADHD even when he or she does not show any sign of hyperactivity. Such children suffer from the **"predominantly inattentive" type of ADHD in which** the **child finds it difficult**

to pay attention and often misses out on important details.

Myth 9: ADHD is associated with excessive sugar consumption

Truth: If your child eats more sugar, it does not mean that he or she will develop ADHD. There is no scientific theory or research that suggests the same. Sugar does not impact the area and the size of the parts of the brain that malfunction in the ADHD patients.

Myth 10: Child having trouble focusing means that he or she has ADHD

Truth: Concentration problems might result because of a number of reasons, including anxiety, depression, lack of sleep, stress and no physical activity. A child who finds it difficult to focus has ADHD only when he or she shows more than six symptoms of inattention.

In this chapter, you examined some of the common myths associated with ADHD and the truth about each one of them. To help your child face the disorder or for you to manage your personal and profession life while living with this condition, it is important to get rid of the stereotypes and notions associated with ADHD.

Chapter 7: Know The Signs Of Adhd To Better Help Your Child

Everyone probably knows of a neighbor's kid who is perpetually moving about, or a child's classmate who appears to tune out whatever the teacher says and cannot seem to follow clearly spelled out instructions, or a relative's child who tends to utter out-of-place comments during the most awkward situations. People may think these kids are always making trouble or call them undisciplined, but the truth is that they may have ADHD (attention deficit hyperactivity disorder). Because of their condition, these kids are simply unable to keep their spontaneous responses (attentiveness, speech, and movement) under control.

A child with ADHD usually shows signs and symptoms before he is 7 years old, making it difficult to tell if a child is exhibiting the condition or is simply being a normal kid. As a parent, you may decide that your child does not have ADHD if the signs that you see are few or if his symptoms occur only in certain situations. But you have to pay more attention to your child if he shows several signs and symptoms of ADHD in all situations. You will only be able to figure out the best course of action to take in managing your child's condition once you are truly aware of his issues and struggles.

Silver Lining

Admittedly, ADHD in children can be a challenge for parents. But the condition is associated with the following positive effects/traits too:

Drive and energy: A child with ADHD has the motivation to play or work and win. Because of this intense drive and energy, his parents may find it difficult to divert his attention to other tasks.

Spontaneity and enthusiasm: A parent of a child with ADHD could never say that he or she has a boring child, especially when the child has lots of interests that he is enthusiastically willing to share with others. Exasperating or not, children with ADHD are certainly loads of fun.

Flexibility: Due to their tendency to be interested in more than one thing at the same time, children with ADHD have a more open mind when it comes to new ideas. This makes it easy for them to consider other alternatives.

Creativity: A child with ADHD could never be called unimaginative or deemed uninspired. Being a daydreamer who has several ideas brewing in his head all at once, it is but natural for him to be an expert in problem solving or to be creative in everything he does.

Different Peas of the Same Pod

Some kids with ADHD have a hyperactive nature, are constantly on the move and are inevitably disrupting everyone they come across. On the other hand, there are other kids with ADHD who just sit still and keep quiet, with their minds a million miles away.

One child with ADHD may spend too much time on the task at hand, and his parents would be hard pressed to get him to work on other things. But another child with ADHD may hardly pay attention to a task and suddenly decide to do something else that catches his fancy.

There are 3 main ADHD characteristics, namely hyperactivity, impulsivity, and inattention. It is a matter of which of these characteristics predominate that determines what signs and symptoms may be observed in a child with ADHD:

Hyperactive, impulsive, and attentive

Hyperactive, impulsive, and inattentive

Inattentive, not hyperactive, and not impulsive

Because they do not disrupt anyone, it is too easy to overlook kids with ADHD who only show symptoms of inattentiveness. But, these same symptoms lead these kids to trouble because they do not follow directions, do not perform their best in school, or fail to play any game by the rules.

Adults tend to expect little kids to be naturally hyperactive and easily distractible, which is why what they usually notice in preschoolers with ADHD are the dangerous climbs, uttered insults, and other impulsive actions. By the time most kids reach 4 or 5 years old, they have already learned about the importance of sitting in silence when told to, not blurting anything that comes to their minds, and paying attention to other people. This is why by the time kids are going to school, the ones with ADHD stand out with the symptoms of the 3 main characteristics (hyperactivity, impulsivity, and inattention).

Hashing Out the Signs of ADHD

1. Hyperactivity

This is ADHD's most easily noticeable sign. Even if many kids are normally active, those with ADHD hyperactivity symptoms are constantly on the move. These kids tend to attempt doing many things at the same time, which drives them to jump around from one task to another. If an adult instructs them to sit still, they tend to respond by drumming their fingers, shaking their legs, or tapping their feet.

The following hyperactivity symptoms are also observed in kids with ADHD:

Having trouble with relaxing or playing quietly

Excessive talking

Constant squirming and fidgeting

Inappropriate running or climbing

Having a quick temper

2. Impulsiveness

Issues with self-control can result from the impulsiveness of kids with ADHD. With less tendency to scrutinize themselves compared to other kids, they usually take up another person's space, ask too personal questions, interrupt a conversation, ask one irrelevant question after another in class, and make thoughtless observations.

Being instructed to wait for a while or to be patient can be extremely difficult for kids with ADHD to follow. Being moody and overreacting in an emotional manner can also be observed in children with impulsiveness signs of ADHD. This is why they are usually viewed by others as weird, needy, or disrespectful.

Different signs of impulsiveness are shown by children with ADHD, including the following:

Tendency to say inappropriate things at inopportune times

Acting on impulse

Intruding on games or conversations of other people

Guessing the solution to a problem instead of trying to solve it

Blurting out answers without letting the teacher finish the question

Failure to control his emotions

3. Inattentiveness

Far from being unable to pay attention, kids with ADHD can easily concentrate on tasks or actually enjoy listening about topics that they find interesting. The trouble is when they come across boring or repetitive tasks or topics, which cause them to immediately tune out. Another problem that kids with ADHD have is staying on track with the things they are involved in. They usually jump from one task to another without finishing a single one. If they do finish ones task, it is usually because they skipped certain steps in the process. They find it more difficult to organize their time when it comes to doing school work than most kids do. Another symptom that one usually observes in children with ADHD is their difficulty in focusing on anything if other things are taking place in their surroundings. This is the reason they typically require somewhere calm and quiet to be able to focus on any task at hand.

The following are the inattentiveness symptoms in kids with ADHD:

Appearing to tune out the person talking to him

Failing to remember and follow instructions

Making careless mistakes as a result of leaving out important details

Leaving tasks unfinished due to boredom

Finding difficulty with planning, organizing, and completing assignments

Losing books, papers, and toys

Chapter 8: Behavioral Therapy For The Child

Many researches have proved that behavioural therapy can work well for a child with ADHD. The parents and teachers should enforce certain rules on the child and explain the consequences of his good and bad behaviour. This will help the child to modify his behaviour for his own good and well- being.

Giving the child clear instructions and rules

It is important that you set some simple rules for the child. Kids with ADHD need regular and consistent monitoring. You should make the kid follow certain rules, but it is important that he understands those rules first.

The child should understand how he should behave and how he shouldn't. Make a set of rules that he is expected to follow. For example, the rules to follow on the dining table. You should write down all the rules and should make sure that the written rules are accessible to him.

Kids with ADHD follow a system of organisation. They should know the consequences of following or not following the rules. Try to make the system as clear and transparent as possible. It is also important that you follow the system you have set out for the child. If you've promised something for certain behaviour, make sure you fulfil your promise.

Positive reinforcement

The kids with ADHD receive so many complaints about their behaviour that it is important that they get an environment of love and positivity at home. You have to make sure that the kid feels loved. He should be treated as an equal to his siblings.

Whenever the kid does something good, you need to appreciate him. Appreciation will go a long way in helping the kid with ADHD. You can do something simple, such as giving him a hug or a smile.

Simple gestures and appreciation can help to improve the impulse control of the kid. If he completes a task that you asked him to, praise him and tell him how good he is. Help him to believe in himself. Even if you have something negative to tell him, watch your words and actions. Be as polite with him as possible. He needs love more than anything else.

Rewarding the child for good behaviour

When possible, you should reward the kids frequently and should also keep changing the kind of rewards you give. Kids with ADHD will get bored easily so you need to keep them interested.

You can keep a chart hanging on the kid's wall. You could mark stars for the kid's good behaviour throughout the week. This visual mechanism will keep the child interested throughout the week.

Try to reward with certain activities rather than a toy.

Don't make false promises. Reward them on the day you promised.

You can keep weekly as well as monthly rewards. This way the child has a small term goal and also a long term goal.

Teaching the child to make friends by improving his social skills

It is a known fact that children with ADHD feel a little awkward socially. They often find it very difficult to interact socially. While they struggle with their interactions, they come across as kids who are very aggressive and who speak too much.

You should understand that it might be difficult for other kids of their age to understand your kid's condition. Your kid might become an easy target for the kids of his age. This, in return, will hamper his self-confidence further.

Many of the kids with ADHD are known to be extremely creative and intelligent. But, they might take time to adjust socially. You, as a guardian, need to help your kid through this journey. You need to help them until they are capable enough to make social interactions.

These kids find it difficult to fit in a group and to make friends. It is naturally difficult for them to understand the social rules and norms. They lack the social skills to converse smoothly in a group of people. It is important that the kid is helped to be a better listener. With time and continuous efforts, he should be able to understand the body language of different people.

You can help a kid with ADHD to improve his social interactions in the following ways:

First and foremost, you should step in to choose the right playmates for your kids. As a small kid, he will be unable to choose the right companions for himself. It is important that he spends his time and energies with the right kind of people.

You should be very careful about which friends you invite to play with him. You should invite 2-3 playmates at a time.

You should watch the child while he plays with his playmates. Though you should not intervene and the child should not know of your presence, you should make sure that there is no hitting and yelling.

When the child is old enough to understand his challenges, you should have a direct talk with him. It is important that you are gentle in your ways, but at the same time it is important that you are clear and honest with the kid.

To make him more comfortable in a group, you can play a fun game with him where you pretend to be him and he pretends to be someone else, and then you can trade roles. Such games will be fun and will help the kid to get used to such social scenarios.

Your child should understand what a good behaviour is. He should know when he misbehaves. You should reward him for his good behaviour.

Chapter 9: How To Deal With Having A Child With Adhd

A kid with ADHD can get to be disappointed by grown-ups and peers who treat them contrastingly due to the way their brain works, adding to their everyday battles. Legitimate treatment, in any case, helps a greater number of kids with ADHD do well. That is the reason it is vital to teach yourself about your kid's ADHD and how to treat it.

Remember that not the slightest bit or shape is your kid idiotic or crazy. Their brain is wired in an unexpected way, keeping in mind they can be a significant modest bunch, they are not idiotic or insane.

Instruct yourself. As a guardian, you are your kid's most imperative counselor. That is the reason why you have to end up knowledgeable on your kid's therapeutic, lawful, and instructive rights.

Get your kid analyzed by a specialist if they have not been as of now. Specialists can figure out your kid has ADHD or not taking into account standard rules. They will likewise take a gander at your kid's therapeutic history and screen affirmations about your kid's conduct from instructors and care givers. Once your kid has a diagnosis, your specialist can tell if a pharmaceutical regimen is the right answer.

Get some information about your kid's diet regimen. While it is still indistinct whether an adjustment in eating routine can help with ADHD indications, there are a few specialists who trust that high protein nourishments and complex carbs can enhance attention. Simply ensure that you run any real eating routine changes by a specialist first.

Ensure that both you and your kid are instructed about ADHD and your treatment alternatives. Your kid's treatment arrangement may incorporate treatment, custom curriculum projects and medications. Studies demonstrate that a blend of treatment and drug creates positive results over treatment alone.

Go to care groups. Care groups will interface you to different families with comparable encounters and concerns.

Go to child rearing aptitudes training. Kids with ADHD may not react well to routine child rearing practices, which is the reason specialists prescribe parenting skills. Parental skill training will demonstrate you how to change your youngster's conduct using prizes and results.

Give positive input to the conduct you need to support and overlook conduct you need to dissuade. At the point when conduct turns out to be truly crazy, consider placing them in a time out. Create a graph that tracks your kid's objectives and accomplishments. Reward your kid when they meet their objectives.

Be clear and predictable when conveying the guidelines to your kid. Maintain a strategic distance from indulgent clarifications.

Participate in charming or unwinding exercises with your kid.

Help your kid find what they do well.

Be sure and acclaim your kid's great focuses.

Rebuild circumstances so they are more sensible for somebody with ADHD. This could mean constraining the quantity of mates to maintain a strategic distance from over incitement or separating a major assignment into smaller, more sensible tasks.

Investigate getting an ADD mentor for your youngster. Including mentors can help your kid be more effective. In the event that you cannot engage an ADD mentor, consider including someone to help with a specific territory your kid battles with, for example, an expert coordinator.

Consider social aptitudes coaching as this may educate your kid practices which will help them create and keep up social connections.

Make an everyday calendar and keep the same day by day routine from wake-up time to sleep time. Ensure you incorporate homework, and additionally indoor and open air activities. Keep the everyday plan some place in the house, for example, a notice board or the fridge. This can help your youngster keep focused.

Limit TV time. While there is not an unmistakable connection between TV and ADHD, specialists suggest that more established kids observe close to two hours of TV a day. Urge your kid to take an interest in exercises that foster attention abilities, for example, recreations, riddles, and reading.

Request that your kid's school check whether your kid is qualified for an individualized education program. Some ADHD kids fit the bill for individualized education programs as per the rules put forward in the Individuals with Disabilities Act. Consider enlightening educators concerning your kid's ADHD toward the beginning of every school year.

Chapter 10: Tips For Dealing With Adhd In Children

Managing ADHD in children is difficult. It can make you irate, disappointed and depleted. Here are some useful tips for guardians.

As a matter of first importance, you have to deal with yourself. On the off chance that you are not in the best of wellbeing, you will be more emotional and you won't have the vitality it brings to stay aware of your child. Dealing with your wellbeing implies eating right, practicing consistently, resting soundly and setting aside opportunity to de-push.

A solid eating routine is imperative for you and your child. Attempt to get the garbage sustenance out of the house. Eat more foods grown from the ground. Attempt to get several servings of greasy fish like fish or salmon consistently. Not exclusively is fish solid, it is additionally rich in omega-3 unsaturated fats, which are here and there valuable for children with attention shortfall disorders.

Your child needs heaps of physical movement to smolder off steam and lessen hyperactivity. It will likewise help both of you rest soundly on the off chance that you get loads of work out. Go for an energetic stroll in the morning. Circled the yard toward the evening before it's the ideal opportunity for homework.

In the event that your child is mature enough, consider a game like b-ball or soccer, yet not softball. There is a lot down time, which is not useful when managing children with ADHD.

Aikido and other combative technique are now and again great decisions, the length of the child appreciates the preparation. You might have the capacity to take a yoga class in the meantime and yoga lessens push.

Resting soundly can be hard both for guardians and for hyperactive children. Early, standard sleep times alongside following an all around arranged routine regularly will offer assistance.

Take no less than a hour prior to sleep time to kill the TV and locate a peaceful movement. Shading or perusing books is a decent decision. You can shading, as well. It's exceptionally unwinding and being casual is essential for managing children with ADHD.

It recalls that your child is normally not getting things done to disturb you deliberately. Having an attention shortage disorder can be similarly as disappointing, debilitating and aggravating as attempting to manage somebody who has one.

Burn through 10 or 15 minutes nestling with your child before his or her sleep time. This is important quality time that helps you two reconnect, particularly following a contention amid the day.

Assist is accessible for managing ADHD in children. You can join a care group or just converse with an understanding companion. Exploit any help that is accessible. It will make both of you more joyful and more advantageous.

Chapter 11: Strategies For Yourself

If you are the person who has been diagnosed with ADHD, you might be thinking, "OK, now what? I saw my doctor, got some meds and I'm going to see a therapist. But how am I going to get through my day?" The answer is: setting yourself up for success. You have to structure your world in a way that works with the way your brain works.

At Home

Strategy #1: Get Organized

Disorganization is arguably the biggest challenge adults with ADHD face. The inattention and distractibility make keeping up with things difficult if left unchecked. Getting organized can feel like a monumental task. It is doable! The key is to make a plan – keep it simple - and break it down into small steps. Here are a few tips for getting started:

- Create Physical Space

One thing we know about clutter is that clutter increases stress. Creating a clean, organized visual space encourages feelings of calm. Taking it a room or even a closet at a time, enlist the help of a friend and start creating your space. Remove what you're not using anymore. Get some boxes or bins for the things you use frequently or need easy access to like keys or important papers. Get in the habit of putting things where they go. The important thing is to find a logical place for everything so that you know where it is when you need it and it is out of your way when you're not using it. How you organize your space is less important than the fact that it is organized in a way that makes sense to you.

- Write It Down

Don't lull yourself into thinking you can keep important events, dates and things to do in your head. That's not an ADHD thing. That's a human thing. Our short-term memories can only hold a limited amount of information at any given time.

Calendars and to-do lists are a great way to keep up with what you've done and what you need to do next. You can use a paper lists and calendars or check out any one of the many smart phone apps out there. An advantage of using an app is that you don't have to worry about losing a list or your calendar.

Strategy #2: Become a Clock Watcher

An hour is an hour. For a person with ADHD, though, the perception of time is different. Being on time to appointments, finishing time-limited tasks and estimating how long a task might take can be challenging. The key to managing time better is to become more aware of time. How do you do that? Use a clock or watch. Make sure to check the time, especially when you are getting ready to start a task.

- Use timers

Inattention and distractibility can make time-limited activities more challenging. Timers are great to use when you only have a certain amount of time to get something done. They provide accurate

71

feedback on passage of time and can help focus your attention back on the task at hand.

- Give Yourself Extra Time

People with ADHD have difficulty estimating the time it will take to do something. If you have an appointment, plan to leave a few minutes earlier than you think you need to. If you have a task to do, give yourself extra time. A good rule of thumb is for every 30 minutes you think a task will take, add 10 minutes. When considering travel time, count backwards from your departure time not your arrival time.

At Work

Poor time management, difficulty prioritizing tasks, poor job performance, chronic tardiness and other job-related problems are often struggles for adults with ADHD. Remember executive functioning from chapter 1? Turns out, these problems are all related to problems with EF. EF tells you whether you're doing what you're supposed to be doing, whether you're getting things done appropriately and whether you're on time or late to a meeting. Poor EF explains why a person with ADHD can waste hours on a minor task or get distracted by someone walking by their office door. It's why their desk looks like a mountain of debris and that important file is nowhere to be found. It's not intentional but it is nonetheless a problem in the workplace. So what's an employee with ADHD to do?

Strategy #3: Set Yourself Up For Success

This means setting up your workspace so that you maximize productivity and minimize distractions. Two of the biggest culprits in workplace success for people with ADHD are distraction and time management.

- Be A Distraction Buster

Distractions can be internal or external. Internal distractions are things like daydreaming or having a "brilliant idea" in the middle of completing a report your boss needs in 15 minutes. Keep a notepad nearby and jot the idea down for later.

External distractions are things like phones ringing or people walking by. If you are lucky enough to have an office, close your door, use a "Do Not Disturb" sign or let your calls go to voice mail for a set period of time. If you are in a more open area, turn your desk to the wall.

- Manage Your Time

When it comes to time management, structure is key. Having a set, prioritized daily schedule can help keep you on track. Take a few minutes each morning to look at the day ahead and make sure you have your tools ready. Think twice before impulsively adding anything on. It's OK to say no or at least, "Let me check my schedule and get back to you." That phrase will give you time to think it through.

Strategy #4: Coach Me Up!

Meds and therapy and lifestyle changes are great. Sometimes what's needed is support. Enter ADHD coaches. More and more, people with ADHD are turning to coaches to help them find new ways to manage their worlds more efficiently. ADHD coaches are specially trained to help people with ADHD. Coaches offer guidance and accountability, checking in periodically to see how things are going. The idea is for the person to "internalize" new skills and learn to monitor their own behavior.

Chapter 12: How To Cope With Your Adhd Child

As you have probably already figured out since you are reading this book is that parenting children with ADHD is not the same as parenting other children. You have probably seen that most common parenting tasks turn into major battles with your ADHD child, such as getting them to sleep at night or getting them out the door in the morning. All those things you take for granted with your other children turns into a daily struggle.

In order to cope with these daily struggles you have probably looked everywhere for help, from reading article after article online to talking to a slew of people about things that might work. The problem is with ADHD children there is no one way that is right in terms of parenting and this is because all ADHD children are different. As a parent you need to try a variety of different parenting techniques to see what works for you and your child and what doesn't.

With that being said let's go over a few parenting techniques that other parents have found to be quite successful.

Structure

Children with ADHD thrive on structure; they love to have a daily schedule to follow. Problems often occur when you deviate from the schedule, their brains have a harder time adapting to change. To help make your life, as well as your child's life easier, create a daily routine for your child and then follow that routine every day. Even the simplest rituals, such as laying out clothes the night before, can help create the structure your child craves. Creating a routine is important, but what is even more important is not deviating from that routine. Children with ADHD need consistency, they respond best when they know what to expect. Straying from the routine can lead to chaos, so once you have found a routine that works stick with

it and life for you and your child will be
easier to manage.

Break   up   tasks
One of the biggest problems children with
ADHD have is that they cannot always
remember what they are supposed to do.
You can give them a list of things to do and
chances are they will remember the first
and last thing you told them, but
everything in between went in one ear
and out the other. Breaking down tasks
into smaller tasks makes things more
manageable for your child, but trying to
remember everything they are supposed
to do can still be overwhelming. To help
with this you can create a chart that
breaks down all of their tasks. The chart
allows them to see what they have done
and what is still left.

Organization
One of the daily struggles your child will
face is dealing with everyday life. Often
times the things you take for granted will
overwhelm your child. Many parents find
it beneficial to organize their home in a

way to give their child a break from the chaos surrounding them. Find a nice quiet place inside your home where your child can get away from things. Keeping your home neat can also help, as your child will know where things are supposed to go. It all goes back to creating structure for your child.

Distractions

For children with ADHD distractions are one of hardest areas to deal with. The term "Squirrel" interjected halfway through a conversation is something many of you can identify with. It is the perfect way to describe the mind of a person with ADHD; they are easily distracted by the smallest things. Children in a classroom can become distracted by the sound of pencils scratching across the paper or even a pen dropping on the ground. The inability to focus is made worse by the smallest of distractions. To help your child cope you need to do what you can to limit these distractions. Creating a quiet area in the house can help limit distractions, but so will limiting electronics.

Several studies show that electronics encourage the impulsive behavior in children with ADHD. The funny thing is they might be a distraction from the more important things, but they can also help your child to focus. The constant change found in video games and television shows help keep ADHD children tuned in for longer periods of time, so many parents overlook electronics as being a distraction. The truth is you want to limit your child's use of electronics. Sitting and playing video games doesn't allow that excess energy to be released, which increases the chances of meltdowns.

Regular   Exercise
Children with ADHD have plenty of extra energy, which can make parenting hard. All of that built up energy causes kids to fidget and squirm or even act out at some rather inappropriate times. Regular exercise can help burn off that energy, plus it can also help improve your child's

focus and provides numerous other health benefits. Joining a team sport or just simply playing at the park is a great way to exercise.

Instill good eating habits One of the most common things parents find in children with ADHD is horrible eating habits, more so in children who are on specific medications. Many children, if not monitored, will go hours without eating and then eat a ton once their medication has worn off. These kinds of eating habits can wreak havoc on your child's physical and emotional health. The best thing you can do is create set meal and snack times and stick to them. At meal and snack times always offer healthy choices rather than junk food. Many kids will pick at their food, so parents that are worried about their child not receiving the proper amounts of vitamins and minerals that a growing body needs to develop properly, fix this by adding a vitamin and mineral supplement to their daily diet to give them anything that might be missing.

Teach your child to wait Impulse control is a very hard thing for ADHD children to master; they are constantly speaking out of turn and can barely contain themselves when they have to wait their turn to say something. The problem with this is when they act on their impulses they are not thinking before they speak; they are simply speaking their minds, which can often lead to hurt feelings. As a parent you need to help teach your child how to wait before they speak, giving them time to plan their responses. This is easier said than done, but you can start working with your child by asking them questions about something they enjoy, such as a movie. Ask them the question and tell them to think about their answer before giving it. The more you practice this with them, the easier it will become.

Encouraging them to think out loud can also help with controlling their impulsiveness. Acting out is normal for children with ADHD and most can't control those impulses because self-control is a problem. When your child acts out, talk with them about what they are thinking. Don't get mad at them for acting out, get them to focus on why they did what they did. Ask them what it is they were thinking, so you can help use their thoughts and reasons as a way to help them learn self-control.

Pay attention to how you act
All children, not just children with ADHD, learn by example. Children tend to act and behave based on what they see from the adults around them. If you are constantly yelling that is the same behavior they will exhibit. Sure it can be frustrating dealing with your child's outburst, but you have to pay attention to how you respond to it. Losing your temper is not going to help matters, but if you remain calm it can help calm your child down. The best way to remain calm during your child's meltdowns is to calm yourself first, even if that means stepping away to gain control

of your thoughts and then approach your child.

Something else to pay attention to is how you act towards your child. The things that you say to your child will impact how your child views themselves. Your child doesn't realize how much stress their behavior causes, remember their ADHD is not their fault; it is just the way their brain works. Whenever you are dealing with your child you need to stay positive and encourage them. Believing in your child will set them up for success in the future.

Sleeping

Getting enough sleep each night is hard for adults, but it is even harder for children with ADHD. Most parents whose children have been diagnosed with ADHD will tell you that one of the hardest parts of their day is bedtime, even though doctor's will tell you that medication should help improve sleep patterns, don't hold your breath. Many children with ADHD have a hard time not only falling asleep, but sleeping through the night. This lack of sleep only makes their ADHD symptoms worse. As a parent you need to do everything you can to help your child get the rest that they need. The best way to do this is by limiting stimulants, which includes electronics before bedtime, as well as sugar. Creating a routine to follow at bedtime that encourages relaxation can also help your child wind down.

Counseling

Now this might not be right for everybody, but many parents find it to be truly helpful. Counseling is not going to solve all of your parenting issues, but it is a great resource to turn too. A counselor will help encourage your child in ways that you cannot, but can also provide assistance for you as a parent. They are a great resource to add to your support group. Again, counseling is not something everybody will use, but it shouldn't be discarded without thinking about it first.

Chapter 13: Gather Everything Before Starting

Gather everything you will need before starting a task. The whole point, is to not have to get up and lose focus on whatever we are doing. Before starting the task, think about what you will need. Sometimes something happens where we have to get up and thats ok. As long as you try to have everything together before starting. You will see a huge difference in the amount of work you can get done without losing focus.

You don't have to write a list out and waste a lot of time preparing. Just mentally go through what you will need for whatever it is your are doing. Most of the time you will have to go get something. But that's better than constantly getting up to look for something. This comes back to being organized. If you have to clean and are organized. All of the cleaning supplies should be in one place. That way you can grab everything and not have to come back and lose focus.

ADHD is conquered by being organized. That really is what your main focus should be. It takes a lot of discipline and will power but it can be done. Just take the extra steps and you will be surprised with the results you get.

Fun Stuff First

I am a firm believer in doing the fun stuff first. The fun stuff is whatever that means to you. I don't mean play a video game for 8 hours and not do something you should have. If you play guitar and usually practice for 30 mins. Do that first and then do your chores or run errands.

I believe that after you accomplish something fun. Your brain will want more. And the harder tasks will be easier to focus on. Make sure you have a timer for the fun stuff. Being the way we are makes it extremely easy to lose track of time and only get one thing done. A phone alarm works perfectly for these situations. Set it for however long you want to work on whatever you are doing. Then when it goes off, instantly stop and move on to the next task.

You run a high chance of losing track of time if you don't stop when the timer goes off. It's the same thing as closing your eyes when the alarm goes off in the morning. There is a very high chance that you over sleep and run late for whatever it is you are doing that day.

Take Breaks During Transitions

After completing a task, give your brain 5 or 10 minutes to recharge. Take a walk, do some yoga, pushups or something to relax for a few minutes. Meditation has done wonders for a lot of people with ADHD. We just need something to allow our brains to rest. Our brains need time after focusing for long periods.

You will notice a major difference when you start your next task after a nice break. Just make sure to actually start the next task. I know it is hard to start again. You have to constantly hold yourself accountable.

Go into your mental break, knowing that you are about to start your next task. If you are already in the mood for work, it wont be as hard to start the next task. After some trial and error, you can adjust the time for your breaks. You may learn that you don't need as long as someone else. Or you may find that you need a little longer than another person.

As i said previously, everyone is different and require a different set of guidelines. These are just a skeleton for you to make your own schedule and guide.

Split Up Larger Tasks

There is always the constant threat of distraction. Which is why we need to break up large tasks into smaller ones. Rather than working for a specified time, then taking a break. Split up the task into steps. After each step, take a second to collect yourself. Then move on to the next step.

This will keep you from getting overwhelmed and discouraged. The feeling of accomplishing each step will keep the momentum up. Which will in turn, make it easier to complete. If you feel even the smaller task is too much. Break it down into an even smaller task. If you do this, the bigger task will be done without you even realizing.

It is very easy to get overwhelmed if you aren't careful. Especially on a large task where it seems that it will never get done. You build a home brick by brick, not wall by wall. Stay focused on the small, micro tasks, and they will build up to a bigger task. Before you know it the whole thing will be done and you will have that feeling of accomplishment that makes us all feel like a million bucks.

Chapter 14: Adhd Treatment Options

ADHD is a disorder that affects the brain and behaviors. There's no known cure for ADHD, but several options can help your child manage their symptoms.

Treatments range from behavioral intervention to prescription medication. In many cases, medication alone is an effective treatment for ADHD. However, the National Institute of Mental Health suggests that including other options is important.

Stimulant and nonstimulant medications

Medication is often an important part of treatment for a child with ADHD. However, it can be a difficult decision to make as a parent.

To make the best choice, you and your child's doctor should work together to decide if medication is a good option. If so, ask the doctor whether your child needs medication during school hours only, or on evenings and weekends as well. You and the doctor should also determine what type of medication might be best. The two main types of ADHD medications are stimulants and nonstimulants.

Central nervous system stimulants

Central nervous system (CNS) stimulants are the most commonly prescribed class of ADHD drugs. These drugs work by increasing the amounts of the brain chemicals called dopamine and norepinephrine. The effect improves your child's concentration and helps them focus better. Common CNS stimulants used to treat ADHD include:

amphetamine-based stimulants (Adderall, Dexedrine, Dextrostat)

dextromethamphetamine (Desoxyn)

dextromethylphenidate (Focalin)

methylphenidate (Concerta, Daytrana, Metadate, Ritalin)

Nonstimulant medications

Your child's doctor may consider nonstimulant medications when stimulants haven't worked or have caused side effects that your child finds hard to handle.

Certain nonstimulant medications work by increasing levels of norepinephrine in your child's brain. Norepinephrine is thought to help with attention and memory. These nonstimulant treatments include:

atomoxetine (Strattera)

antidepressants like nortriptyline (Pamelor)

Other nonstimulant medications can also help with ADHD. It isn't fully known how these medications help with ADHD, but there is some evidence that they help certain chemicals work better in the part of the brain involved with attention and memory. These other nonstimulants include:

guanfacine (Intuniv)

clonidine (Kapvay)

Side effects of stimulants and nonstimulants

The more common side effects of stimulants and nonstimulants are pretty similar, although they tend to be stronger for stimulants. These side effects can include:

headache

trouble sleeping

stomach upset

nervousness

irritability

weight loss

dry mouth

The more serious side effects of these drug types are rarer. For stimulants, the serious side effects in children can include:

hallucinations (seeing or hearing things that aren't there)

increased blood pressure

allergic reaction

suicidal thoughts or actions

For nonstimulants, the serious side effects in children can include:

seizures

suicidal thoughts or actions

Therapeutic ADHD treatments

Several therapy options can help children with ADHD. Talk to your doctor about whether one or more of these options would be a good choice for your child.

Psychotherapy

Psychotherapy can be useful in getting your child to open up about their feelings of coping with ADHD. ADHD can cause your child to have problems with peers and authority figures. Psychotherapy can help children better handle these relationships.

In psychotherapy, a child may also be able to explore their behavior patterns and learn how to make good choices in the future. And family therapy can be a great way to help figure out how best to work through disruptive behaviors.

Behavior therapy

The goal of behavior therapy (BT) is to teach a child how to monitor their behaviors and then change those behaviors appropriately. You and your child, and perhaps the child's teacher, will work together. You'll develop strategies for how your child behaves in response to certain situations. These strategies often involve some sort of direct feedback to help the child learn suitable behaviors. For instance, a token reward system could be devised to support positive behaviors.

Social skills training

Social skills training can sometimes be useful if a child shows serious issues dealing with social environments. As with BT, the goal of social skills training is to teach the child new and more appropriate behaviors. This helps a child with ADHD play and work better with others. A therapist may try to teach behaviors such as:

waiting their turn

sharing toys

asking for help

dealing with teasing

Support groups

Support groups are great for helping parents of children with ADHD connect with others who may share similar experiences and concerns. Support groups typically meet regularly to allow relationships and support networks to be built. Knowing you're not alone in dealing with ADHD can be a huge relief for many parents.

Support groups can also be a great resource for ideas and strategies for coping with your child's ADHD, especially if your child was recently diagnosed. Ask your doctor how to find support groups in your area.

Parenting skills training

Parenting skills training gives you tools and techniques for understanding and managing your child's behaviors. Some techniques may include the following:

Immediate rewards: Try using a point system or other means of immediate rewards for good behavior or work.

Timeouts: Use a timeout when your child becomes too unruly or out of control. For some children, being pulled out of a stressful or overstimulating situation can help them learn how to react more appropriately the next time a similar situation comes up.

Togetherness: Find time together every week to share a pleasurable or relaxing activity. During this time together, you can look for opportunities to point out what your child does well and praise their strengths and abilities.

Striving for success: Structure situations in a way that allows your child to find success. For instance, you might allow them to have only one or two playmates at a time so they don't get overstimulated.

Stress management: Use methods such as meditation, relaxation techniques, and exercise to help manage stress.

Behavioral interventions for home and school

One of the biggest concerns for parents of children with ADHD is their child's success in school. A lot of that success depends on how organized they are. Being organized is a skill that many children with ADHD struggle with. Simple steps such as these below can be an immense help.

Build a schedule

Set the same routine every day. Try to make sure that waking up, bedtime, homework, and even playtime are done at consistent times. Post the schedule in a visible place. If a change must be made, make it as far in advance as possible.

Organize everyday items

Make sure that clothing, backpacks, school supplies, and play items all have a designated, clearly marked space.

Use homework and notebook organizers

Stress the importance of writing down assignments and bringing home anything needed to complete homework.

Ask about using a computer in class

For some children with ADHD, handwriting is another obstacle to success. If necessary, see if their teacher will allow for computer use in the classroom.

Use positive reinforcement

Children with ADHD often receive criticism from authority figures. Then they start to expect it. If they get only negative feedback without ever hearing positive things about themselves, they'll start to think of themselves as bad.

To boost your child's self-esteem and reinforce appropriate behavior, use positive reinforcement. If your child follows the rules and behaves well, give small rewards and praise. This lets them know what behavior you prefer, while letting them know that they can be good.

Talk with your doctor

Effective treatment for a child's ADHD often includes several approaches. These can include medication and one or more types of therapy, as well as behavioral measures that you can put into practice as a parent. Getting proper treatment can help your child manage their ADHD symptoms and feel better about themselves.

To learn more about what treatment might work best for your child, talk with your child's doctor. Some of your questions might include:

Would medication, therapy, or both help my child?

Would you recommend a stimulant or a nonstimulant medication or my child?

What side effects from the medication should I watch for?

Chapter 15: Attention Deficit Disorder: What Is It Anyway?

As parents, I am sure that many of you will have spent sleepless nights concerned that the strange behavior our child exhibited today may be the first signs of Attention Deficit Disorder. Our concerns are justified in many ways as most of us believe we know the fundamental signs of the disease are, and we obviously panic at the thought we might have to deal with it.

The fear of the disease, its effects and the way it will impact on the family is only one part of it. There is often an underlying guilt that in some way our actions may be responsible for this having happened. Most of us will in some way or another blame ourselves, believing that we have not been strict enough or applied enough discipline, or conversely that we have been too strict. While these apprehensions may be quite normal the ideas aren't always rational or well-founded.

There are usually assed to be three broad stages in any normal childhood development;

The first is observable in babies / infants. During this stage infants become focused on and preoccupied with certain objects to the exclusion of what else is around them. If a kid's development stalls around this point it may later show as signs of autism.

In the second recognizable stage, which is observed in older children, the child becomes interested in a range of things at the same time and they then become incapable of concentrating or focusing on any one thing or action for any length of time. This is the key to ADD, as if the child stalls in their development at this stage they may later in their childhood go on to suffer Attention Deficit Disorder (ADD).

The third stage assists a child to mature to a point from which they can comfortably focus and voluntarily apply their attention in one certain direction for longer periods of time. They can then alter their focus or actions as and when they have a need to.

This stage is therefore a crucial transitional stage which moulds a child for success in the classroom and in the real world.

But ADD does not only make a child or young adult incapable of focusing. It also reduces their ability to take decisions. They can then become indecisive even in normal everyday life. An

Understanding And Treating ADHD

example may be that they become disoriented when crossing a road and turn back into on- coming traffic, or lose the reason why they were crossing in the first place.

At the opposite end of the scale, ADD sufferers can also become totally focused on a specific object or task. They can become consumed by it and are as a result are absolutely cut-off and oblivious to everything else. an example of this manifesting is that they may watch the same movie again and again without realizing, or read a certain part of a book repeatedly with no reaction or loss of concentration. Later in life this behavior might turn into over-eating or substance-abuse or other compulsive behavior.

Another increasingly reported variation of ADD is Attention Deficit Hyperactivity Disorder known as ADHD. This leads to sufferers always needing to stay busy, moving from place to place or being unable to slow down. It is increasingly being diagnosed in young teenagers. This can drive parents mad and keep them up nights in an attempt to calm their child and entice them to sleep. These children and young adults will find it difficult to switch off but they can experience many of the events above. While experience of this type of patient has led Psychologists to conclude that ADD is not a problem that a child will grow out of naturally they have also quite strongly rejected any link with the parent causing this disorder. There is no direct causal relationship between what a parent does an how likely a child is to develop ADD or ADHD. So if your child is suffering from ADD stop blaming yourself, instead recognize the problem for what it is and contact a specialist as soon as possible.

Understanding And Treating ADHD

ADD: How Does It Affect Your Child's Schooling And Education?

There is no doubt that it is a difficult task to teach any child, but more so one suffering from Attention Deficit Disorder. A significant number of schools have identified ADD as a legitimate problem and have ADDressed the issue with changes in teaching methods. Substantial developments and improvements have been made in methodology to recognize the disorder, but there are still some which lag behind in arrangements and cannot answer an individual's needs.

The way in which ADD can influence a classroom is often seen even before a diagnosis has been made. It might be observed in a child reacting to his classmates, as physical reactions such as snatching books, or in a child sitting in a corner, her mind elsewhere.

It is often a teacher who recognizes that a student is having problems attending to lessons or are over-active. But identifying the problem is just the first step, the most difficult thing is changing the behavior.

The treatment of ADD can only start once everyone acknowledges it. Then a diagnosis has to be made before a course of treatment is agreed. It is important early in the day to decide if medicine as a method is required, since this will determine the course of any treatment. There are some schools, which insist that a child suffering with ADD be given medicines to mitigate the effects. Some schools, however take a more patient stance and are wiling to comply with the parent's wishes.

In an ideal world, your child should be in a school which understands the effectiveness that working together as part of a team causes, by the school administration taking involvement in your child's circumstances and respecting decisions as a parent. This will assist your child in achieving the best that they can.

Regrettably some schools do not have such an open-minded vision. Communities which are smaller, and places which are poorer relative to other districts may have a habit of being too conservative. These schools can sometimes lag in catering to children who have a special need or suffer from a specific situation.

Understanding And Treating ADHD

ADD does make some children harder to teach. They are often more chaotic and more difficult to control. For these reasons a few schools refuse to take on and accommodate such potentially unruly children. Regardless of this you must make sure that no child is provided with a sub-standard, second-rate treatment under any circumstances.

As well as the above, some schools may run remedial classes, or classes only for students with learning issues. Rather than these classes always assisting such children, they can be disadvantaged by this. Children with ADD are not necessarily less intelligent at all, but classes such as these are often of mixed abilities.

Remember though that you are the parent. You have the responsibility to achieve the best for your child. You should always be there for him or her. If any decision taken by the school of the class teacher goes against what you perceive to be the well-being or the best education for your child, you should immediately discuss it with them. You may be able to come to a better plan that will ensure the best for your child.

Chapter 16: Strategies For Dealing With Adhd

First of all, there is no hard and fast cure for ADHD. At best, it may be something that your child grows out of over time. However, ADHD may be a constant presence in your child's life and affect them well into adulthood. Many parents seek to "fix" the ADHD. Make peace with the fact that this isn't possible for you to do and focus your energies on helping your child learn how to, recognize their triggers, deal with their emotions and how to live a productive, happy life.

It is common for parents to turn to medication to help alleviate their child's symptoms. As tempting as it might sound to jump straight for the Adderall in the hopes that it will be a quick fix for your child's behavioral struggles, you want to be careful. Adderall is a highly potent amphetamine that stimulates the central nervous system (that part of the brain that is impaired in children with ADHD).

However, as a potent amphetamine, it is highly addictive and comes with host of side effects. When deciding whether or not to expose your child to heavy duty medications, exercise extreme caution.

Therapy is another common strategy for dealing with ADHD, especially in very young children. Therapists will work with children on everything from learning how to take turns to learning how to accurately read facial expressions and similar social cues. However, not everyone has access to this resource. What's more, older children and teenagers may be past the point where direct behavioral conditioning will benefit them.

Luckily, there are plenty of things you can do in the home to help your child navigate the muddy waters of this condition. These strategies come down to two basic categories. First, work with your child not against them. In other words, it won't do to force your child to sit still and pay attention when their body is urging them in another direction. Second, identify triggers and other big-time distractions and eliminate them. In other words, if you know something like TV is a problem, make it not a problem by removing it from the equation or drastically reducing their screen time so they are not overly stimulated.

I want to talk a little more about working with your child's condition. If your child is highly hyperactive, let them run some of that energy out. Enroll them in a sports league or just take them to the park to play. Researchers suggest that exercise, especially aerobic exercise, can be a huge boon when it comes to managing high-energy kids. They also suggest that children who suffer from ADHD and get plenty of exercise will experience better behavior and motor abilities.

Maybe your child isn't the hyperactive kind. There are other ways that you can work with the condition. If your child can't sit still and do a single activity for more than ten minutes, run with this. Shorter activities at a high level of engagement will help your child stay focused on various things without feeling frustrated. You might even try lengthening the time spent on these activities very gradually. However you approach your child's condition, remember that it is a condition. A child isn't going to sit still just because you said so and, when they inevitably don't, it's not because they didn't want to.

Now, let's address the topic of triggers and distractions. Because children with ADHD are wired differently, they are going to react to the modern world a bit differently than your average child might. In other words, televisions, laptops, and tablets are all going to be way too distracting and over stimulating for your child to want to do anything else. If you find it difficult for your son or daughter to focus on school or to go outside and get that much needed exercise because they are glued to your television set, eliminate the television set. Depending on their age and how well they are able to understand what is going on, you may want to assure them that this is not a punishment. By removing the distraction, you are simply trying to help them get better. Pay attention to the unique triggers and distractions that stand in the way of your child's creative and cognitive development and do what you can to limit your child's exposure to them.

One unique aspect of ADHD is hyperfocus. That's right, hyperfocus. Some children with ADHD may become so engrossed in certain activities that it can be next to impossible to tear them away. This may sound like the opposite of ADHD and, for that reason, this behavior may cause some children to have a delayed diagnosis. After all, a child that can draw for hours can't possibly have difficulty with attention and hyperactivity, right? Wrong. Thankfully, there are strategies for dealing with this behavior as well.

Kade, for example, tends to be hyperfocused when he is playing with Legos. As tempting as it is to try and snatch a small break for myself by letting him play until the cows come home, I know that it is important for Kade to learn boundaries. Sometimes those boundaries involve loving limitations when it comes to doing the things we love. I will give him time to work on his projects and gradually bring him away from them with countdowns. I might say, "Buddy, you have fifteen minutes until dinner and you need to put your Legos away." This will be followed by ten and five-minute warnings. This strategy has helped immensely by showing Kade that I respect what he is doing but that I also have expectations of him. What's more, he is given time to process the fact that the Legos will soon need to be put away, making the experience far less jarring than if I were to just walk up to him and say, "put them away now." Employing this strategy will limit your child's frustrations and, ultimately, their outbursts.

In addition to working with your child's needs, eliminating triggers, and setting clear expectations, you can help to improve your child's quality of life through proper nutrition, plenty of sleep, and reliable routines. I'll talk more about these strategies separately as they can have such a strong positive impact on your child's development.

Chapter 17: Common Symptoms Of Adhd

The hallmark symptoms of ADHD include inattention and hyperactivity-impulsivity. Mainly there are three types of ADHD - Combined (symptoms of inattention and hyperactivity-impulsivity) which is the commonest, inattentive ADHD (impaired concentration and attention) and hyperactivity-impulsivity ADHD. For a diagnosis of ADHD, it is important to understand that some symptoms should be present before age seven and there must be some impairment of activities due to the symptoms in more than one sitting like at both home and school.

Inattention

Children suffering from ADHD find it very difficult to pay attention. They are almost always distracted and in the course, distract other children as well. They cannot concentrate and often begin to fantasize about unlikely situations and conditions. It is a little tricky to identify this symptom of ADHD, as the child doesn't run around or show any 'visible' signs of the disorder. However, if you are careful and observant, you will surely be able to detect this ADHD symptom in the child. The symptoms of inattention manifests when the child is faced with a challenging social environment like schooling. The following are the symptoms of inattention:

Difficulty paying attention to details, making careless mistakes in school or other activities, messy and careless work.

Frequent shifts from one incomplete activity to the other.

Procrastination.

Difficulty finishing schoolwork or paperwork or tasks that require concentration.

Inability to maintain attention span on tasks or activities.

Disorganized work habits.

Easy distraction by irrelevant stimuli. Interruption of tasks by trivial noises that others are not paying attention to.

Failure to complete tasks like homework.

Forgetful in daily activities.

Frequent shifts in concentration, not keeping mind on conversations, not listening to others and not following details or rules of activities in social functions.

Hyperactivity

One of the prime symptoms of ADHD is hyperactivity. A child affected by ADHD is most likely to be hyperactive. They cannot sit in one place, find it difficult to control their actions and are constantly distracted due to the reasons mentioned above. Hyperactive children also find it difficult to complete any given task as they cannot sit and complete it and are tempted to get up at all times. These symptoms are always present before the age of seven and include:

Always on the go.

Fidgeting or squirming when seated.

Having to get up often to walk or run around.

Difficulty in playing quietly or engaging in quiet leisure activities.

Running or climbing excessively when it is inappropriate.

Talking excessively.

Impulsivity

Children who suffer from ADHD are usually irresponsible. They say and do things without thinking and without fearing about the consequences. They even find it difficult to wait for the right time to do or say the right things. Symptoms include:

Difficulty in delaying responses.

Impatience.

Difficulty in awaiting turn.

Blurting out answers before question is completed.

Initiating conversations at inappropriate times.

Frequently interrupting or intruding on others.

Watch out for these warning signs of ADHD:

Not listening to instructions.

Excess talking.

Fidgeting, especially hands and feet.

Inability to get organized.

Failure to finish projects.

Difficulty paying attention to and responding to details.

Chapter 18: Managing Everyday Tasks

Living with ADHD means experiencing a variety of difficulties every day. These problems may vary from losing things, forgetting appointments and dates, getting easily distracted, etc. What you are about to read are some simple methods that can aid you in overcoming these difficulties.

Organizing your space

If you want to organize your life, you have to start with organizing some smaller parts and areas of your life. First, take a look at your living space.

Keep all those things that you use on a daily basis and store all those you don't need in bins or closets. Also, things such as your keys, some important documents, bills, or things that you tend to lose frequently should always be stored at the same place.

So, choose on specific place where you will keep these things, make this a rule and stick to it.

Appointment book

After having organized your living space and removed everything that is likely to cause any distractions, buy yourself an appointment book.

Buying this appointment book is not all you have to do, though. When you have this appointment book, you have to make a schedule of all your appointments, tasks or other things you think should be recorded on a weekly or monthly basis.

Then, you have to make a strategy or rule to look at the book a few times a day. Looking at the appointment book is actually studying it, seeing what you have to do next, making a pattern of and preparing for the things to do. Also, make sure to have your book with you whenever you go.

Make your to-do list

The next step is to make your to-do list. This includes a list of things that are not routine things and that really need to be done.

Also, bear in mind that this should not be a long list, as you may feel overwhelmed or confused and then end up finishing nothing. Also, these to-do things may also be steps of something larger.

For instance, you have some big project to finish, be it something personal or something you work on. That project may be broken down into many steps, which you can then add to your to-do list. As with the appointment book, keep your to-do list with you and take a look at it a few times a day.

Make additional lists

You can also make other lists as well. For instance, you can have lists of things of different priority and these lists may be of different colors.

For example, if you take a red list, you can write down things that need to be done urgently. Then, you can have a white list where you can put things that you would like to do or finish in duly time.

You may have one list of the orange, yellow or whatever color you find appropriate that will contain things of medium urgency. So, once you finish something, you can cross it off and thus feel proud of yourself, feel motivated and keep going. Also keep these lists short, and limit them to about 4 or 5 things.

These lists do not serve just to keep you focused and help you not forget things, but they work on another level as well. In other words, when you cross an item or task off that list, you'll feel relief, a sense of accomplishment and satisfaction.

Keep up with your tasks and small steps so as not to let them pile up. If they pile up, it will become overwhelming for you to keep up and you'll do nothing. This will eventually lead you to underestimate yourself, feel depressed, etc.

Make small steps

When making your to-do list or any other additional list, the key is to write only small steps. Why? Because this will keep you focused, you will not get easily distracted, you will consequently feel more motivated and that will keep your morale high.

When you break a project into steps, it allows you to focus on one small step and forget about the others. When you get that one done, you go on with another smaller step leading up to a successfully finished task or project.

For instance, if you have to paint your dog's house, break this down into smaller steps, such as buying paint, preparing the surface for painting, and painting the house.

Use cards for important information

You can have cards of different colors, devising a system to help you organize ideas and things to remember. Besides the card with the things you need to do, you can have a card with some important information, such as phone numbers, passwords, important dates, etc.

You can also have a card with some of your favorite songs, verses, and so on. Or if you are currently working on a project, you can have one card where you can write down some ideas related to the project that come to your mind all of a sudden.

Take advantage of electronic devices

Some people with ADHD find electronic devices very useful, because they can help you remember the things and tasks assigned for a particular day. For instance, you can set alarms to remind you of your appointments, important dates, and other to-do tasks.

Brain training

You can also try to train your brain. For instance, brain games like Sudoku or crossword puzzles may help you improve your otherwise poor concentration, because these activities may stimulate and aid in the creation of new brain cells.

Visualize your day

People suffering from ADHD are said to be creative and to have good visualization skills. That is why it is sometimes suggested to begin each day by visualizing yourself doing all the things you are supposed to do for that day.

However, some people may find it easier and more helpful to focus on or visualize just a few things. Then, they will focus only on these three to five things, and avoid being easily distracted or losing track. These would normally be the things you have on your to-do list.

Summary

What can help you keep up with everyday activities is organizing your living space, using an appointment book, making your to-do list along with any other necessary additional lists, using electronic devices to remember important things, playing brain games to improve concentration, and visualizing your day.

Chapter 19: Alternative Treatments

In this chapter, parents of children with ADD and ADHD, and afflicted adults, will learn about alternative treatments other than medication and psychotherapy intervention.

Over the years, evidence has grown that alternative programs for treating ADD and ADHD can be successful in leading the patient through a more rewarding coping experience. Some of the more effective alternative remedies include biofeedback, meditation and hypnosis, massage and exercise, and the use of herbal supplements.

Biofeedback is the process of using instruments that provide information on the activity of physiological functions. The ECG or electrocardiogram machine is a common example of a biofeedback process in action, measuring the electrical activity of the heart by means of electrodes placed in the torso, wrists, and legs, and giving out results in terms of heart rate, or actually what is called the "interbeat interval." Other devices measure the relative expansion and contraction of the lungs, the amount of oxygenated and unoxygenated blood in the brain, or even electrical activity in the skin.

In one of the available use of biofeedback for the treatment of ADD and ADHD, children are encouraged to play video games, with a controller that can be governed by their brains. In a race car game, for example, the car slows down or comes to a halt when the child's brain waves shift outside of the prescribed appropriate range. As long as they are in the right brain waves, they can drive as fast as they want. The goal in this instance is to effect a permanent change in the abnormal electrical activity in the brain that is associated with ADD and ADHD.

Meditation, the use of guided imagery, and hypnosis can be used in the same was at biofeedback to help calm and focus an impulsive brain. There are certified guided imagery therapists around who can help you with providing your child with imagery and audio tools that can stimulate the subconscious mind and supply it with positive affirmations to resolve the impulsiveness as well as the inattentiveness of the ADD and ADHD-afflicted child.

As for herbal supplements for ADD and ADHD patients, the only herbal remedies that are widely accepted as having a positive effect are herbal teas that encourage a more relaxed sleep. St. John's Wort was popular and used to be a common herbal remedy believed to be effective in dealing with ADD and ADHD among other conditions. The latest research, however, shows that it may have dangerous interactions with prescribed medications. Herbal teas that help the ADD and ADHD patient sleep better include chamomile, lemon grass, spearmint, and other herbs and flowers that induce relaxation and counter restlessness in sleep. Melatonin is also one herbal element that helps initiate sleep for children with ADD and ADHD.

There are not very many studies on the efficacy of herbal remedies, so your best bet would be to seek your doctor's guidance. Don't forget to consult your herbal specialist or naturopath and ask him for more information about remedies that boost brain function. They can help a lot as long as they don't adversely interact with your prescriptions.

Massage and exercise are related alternative remedies, although this may not be the solution for young children, this could be effective for teenagers. A study involving teenage boys with ADD and

ADHD showed it boosted their positive mood and at the same time helped them focus and be more attentive. In fact, the same study showed that the same group of teenage boys had better concentration after receiving 15 minutes of massage for ten consecutive days than those who went through a guided muscle relaxation exercise for the same number of days.

Exercise is always good for the body and the brain. It will improve concentration, will control impulsive behavior. This result happens simply because it induces better blood circulation and therefore distributes nutrients and oxygen well, and gets rid of body wastes faster. Among children with ADD and ADHD, exercise helps them release their energy in a more productive way. There are studies that suggest that a good jog in green open spaces helps boost brain activity, and even a "walk in the park" can make anyone feel better, even those with ADD and ADHD.

Chapter 20: Medical Treatment

Treatment of ADHD means, in all cases, treatment with stimulant medication, which, very frequently, is the only treatment required. There are few interventions in all of medicine that are as quickly and dramatically effective as stimulant medication when used to treat ADHD.

When it works, and it usually does, the child's improve- ment in behavior and functioning, often within days, is almost miraculous, and the child can perform better than he ever has in his life. We have seen this happen again and again and are convinced that failure to treat the ADHD child appropriately represents a terrible lost opportunity.

In some children, this may be the only treatment that is required.

The stimulant medications that are so important in treating ADHD fall into two groups. They are the amphetamines such as Dexedrine, Adderall, and Vyvanse and the methylphenidate compounds such as Ritalin, Methylin, Metadate CD, Ritalin LA, Daytrana, Focalin XR, and Concerta. Amphetamine was introduced in the late 1930s.

Cocerns About Medication

The use of medication to treat children is sometimes upsetting to parents. Parents are troubled for various reasons, and it may be useful to discuss them.

First, many parents have difficulty coming to terms with the fact that their child's behavior problems have a physical rather than a psychological basis; often this is because they find physical problems frightening. They feel that a temper tantrum is soon over, but the chemically abnormal brain may never recover. For this reason, they would rather believe that the problem is psychological. Fortunately, just as with many other serious physical problems, behavior malfunctions with physical origins can sometimes be easily remedied. On the other hand, psychological treatment is not always as effective. For example, some problems of psychological origin cannot be cured despite years of expensive and time-consuming psychological treatment. A child who has been neglected or physically, sexually, or psychologically abused during early childhood may never function normally, even if he later receives warm, considerate parental care and psychotherapy.

A second reason parents sometimes object to treatment with medication is that such treatment seems artificial. To many parents, it does not appear to be a good way to get to the root of the problem. That may be so if the root of the problem is psychological, but in the case of ADHD, it is physical. Because some regulatory functions in the brain are operating less efficiently than usual, chemical means must be used to improve their functioning. Medication can be regarded as a form of replacement therapy; that is, it apparently supplies chemicals that are lacking or decreased or it causes the body to create more of the missing chemicals. At present, we can give no chemical that will permanently cure the deficiency. Medication is necessary unless and until the brain, through its own growth and development, begins producing adequate amounts of the required chemicals.

Stimulant Drug

Stimulant medication for ADHD may be the most effective medication in psychiatry. They are uniquely useful and may turn a child's life around.

Effectiveness

Although both amphetamines and methylphenidate are potentially helpful for children with ADHD, it is impossible to predict how a child will respond to a particular medication. Approximately the same number of children responds to each stimulant, but some children respond well to one medication and not to the other. If one fails, try the other.

However, after careful trials with both drugs, 80–90 percent of children will show a favorable response.

ADHD children generally:

✓ become calmer and less active

✓ develop a longer span of attention

✓ become less stubborn and easier to manage (they "mind" better)

✓ are often more sensitive to the needs of others and much more responsive to discipline and the wishes of others

✓ have longer fuses and fewer or no temper tantrums

✓ experi- ence fewer emotional ups and downs

✓ show a decrease in impulsivity, waiting before they act, and may begin to plan ahead

✓ demonstrate an improvement in school performance (listening, following instructions, completing tasks, getting better grades

✓ improve their handwriting

✓ increase frustration tolerance

✓ become less disorganized

The response of the ADHD child to stimulant medication is frequently a dramatic improvement. At best, most other treatments restore a patient to his previous level of functioning. For example, antidepressants may eliminate a depression, mood stabilizers control the ups and downs of bipolar disorder, and antipsychotics may stop odd thinking and hallucinations, but none allows a person to function better than he ever has before as often happens with stimulants used to treat ADHD.

Dosage

Stimulants are rapidly acting medications, but they come in short-acting and long-acting forms. The short-acting, methylphenidate-based drugs release all the medication at once and may last from 3 to 4 hours, whereas the amphetamine-based drugs may last from 4 to 5 hours.

The long- acting forms gradually release their medication over time and may last from 8 to 12 hours. In the early days, when only the short-acting medications were available, a child might have to take 3–5 doses throughout the day. This could be made to work but usually led to all sorts of social and logistic problems at school and at home. Fortunately, the longer acting forms have been developed (and new ones continue to be developed).

Modern treatment usually begins with a dose of a long- acting medication taken first thing in the morning. It may last all day, which would be ideal. However, it may wear off too soon (for example, before homework is done in the afternoon), so it may need to be supplemented with a dose of a short-acting medication. On the other hand, it may last too long and interfere with sleep, so short-acting forms may be needed instead. The goal is to find the perfect schedule or combination of long and short-acting medication which will cover the waking hours.

Stimulant Medications and Growth

Several years ago, a report was published stating that stimulant medications decreased the rate of growth—both of height and weight—in ADHD children. Since that report appeared, a number of other studies on the same subject have been published. It does appear that growth rate is slowed for a period of one to two years. After that, growth rate appears to become normal, and there seems to be no decreased height among ADHD adolescents. The whole issue is complicated because ADHD children may have growth patterns that are different from those of other children, and the usual tables of growth may not apply to ADHD children. Doctors who have treated ADHD children with stimulants from childhood through adolescence have not observed any long-term effects of stimulant medication on height. If growth slows, it usually rebounds if medication is stopped during summer vacations, although the medication should be restarted if there is significant deterioration in behavior.

There is no doubt that many ADHD children do lose weight on stimulant medication. Although this is sometimes upsetting to parents, there is no information suggesting that it is harmful, and weight usually returns to normal when the medication is stopped. We should re-emphasize that the effects that have been reported are small and that most physicians treating ADHD children regard the psychological benefits as outweighing possible effects on the rate of growth. At a practical level, what the physician must do is follow the child's height, weight, and changes in adjustment and base the use of stimulant medication not only on its effect on growth but on its effect on the child's psychological well-being.

Non-Stimulant Drug

There are several other, nonstimulant drugs occasionally used to treat ADHD that may be useful for a few patients, but they are, without exception, generally much less effective than the stimulants.

Strattera (atomoxetine) is the first nonstimulant medication approved by the FDA for use in ADHD and it is typically taken once daily in the morning. It has a number of bothersome side effects, including sedation, fatigue, decreased appetite, headache, and gastrointestinal upset, which can be sufficiently severe in some people.

Although considerably less effective than the stimulants, it may be the medication to try first on the patients who do not respond to stimulants.

Catapres (clonidine) is a drug developed for the treatment of hypertension (elevated blood pressure) that has been used in treating aggressive ADHD children and as a night-time sedative in children who are receiving stimulants and in whom the stimulants produce insomnia. It has only modest effectiveness and requires two weeks or so for its therapeutic action to begin. It has a number of side effects, including sedation and fatigue, dizziness, constipation, and decreased blood pressure, and it must be stopped slowly because a sudden discontinuation can result in a dangerous blood pressure spike.

Chapter 21: Extraction Of Cbd

There are 4 main methods used to produce or extract CBD from hemp, whole plant extraction, isolate extraction, CO2 extraction and alcohol extraction.

Whole Plant Extraction

The entire hemp plant forms part of the extraction and is one of the more favoured methods. This is because it is believed to be the most effective way to capture the entire cannabinoid spectrum as close to the natural endocannabinoid system as possible

Isolate Extraction

CBD isolates are pure CBD compounds extracted, with their effectiveness dependent on the quality of hemp from which they are derived.

CO2 Extraction

This is when CO2 is forced through the plant to extract the oil, the most complex methods currently available but does allow for the individual cannabinoid compounds to be separated effectively.

Alcohol Extraction

This is the original extraction method used, by soaking the hemp in a solvent to remove the oils after which the solvent is evaporated to leave the CBD oil.

CBD is regarded as a food supplement that helps to bring balance to our bodies and minds by complementing or 'topping up' the endocannabinoid system which most are unable to create enough of therefore causing imbalance.

The human body naturally creates cannabinoids, which are used by the endocannabinoid system to maintain balance/homeostasis within the body. The endocannabinoid system has been long regarded as the most important system in the body for maintaining long term health."

"CBD is one of over 100 cannabinoids found in the cannabis plant. Although CBD has been known to help a myriad of people with different ailments sadly we are unable to promote its health benefits unless it has been tested and approved as a medicinal product.

There are a few products on the market that have this approval such as Epidolex that can be used to treat children with Epilepsy. So far CBD is known to help with not only epilepsy but also anxiety, inflammation, pain relief and sleeping issues.

CBD AND ADHD

CBD is a product of the marijuana (cannabis) plant with the high-inducing THC (tetrahydrocannabinol) compound removed, which means it is not psychoactive. CBD — often in the form of an oil, a tincture, or an edible — has been rumored to reduce anxiety, a common symptom among those diagnosed with ADHD symptoms. No one, though — not even the drug's most hardcore advocates — claims CBD is a treatment for ADHD.

Can CBD oil help you focus?

CBD oil has been shown to positively affect responses to stress and anxiety in individuals by alleviating their symptoms. It has also been shown to help improve brain focus.

When looking at dosage properties and usage recommendations, many sublingual drops recognize on their packaging that while a larger dose might make an individual feel more relaxed and unfocused before bedtime, a smaller dose in the morning can provide a somewhat opposite effect, increasing focus and concentration.

The experiments specifically examining a scientific connection between ADHD and CBD oil are only just entering the early stages. As of yet, there is little specific evidence to prove that CBD oil affects the symptoms of ADHD. However, it is important to note that individuals personally attest to the effectiveness of the oil, and it seems to change from person to person.

Some find it worthwhile to begin their own trial run to discover for themselves how CBD oil might help them. It's important to recognize that one should always consult with a doctor or medical expert prior to beginning any new form of treatment or when they consider dropping any medication.

The effects on the brain are not a new concept. In addition to experiments on focus and brain function, more common studies have started to reveal potential effects on patients with Alzheimer's Disease.

Although still in the early stages, the fact that CBD might be able to slow or reverse certain symptoms of Alzheimer's conditions indicates it's powerful ability to positively strengthen and affect the human brain

Understanding CBD oil and ADHD symptoms

One of the predominant healing factors identified with CBD oil, is its ability to alleviate stress and anxiety. This is one of the indicators supporting its use to lessen ADHD symptoms.

When an individual is diagnosed with ADHD, they find themselves in social, work or school situations requiring certain behaviors. They may struggle to behave in that way and, as a result, experience anxieties about their behavior. CBD oil is capable of alleviating their stress, thereby promoting a healthier mental space allowing them to work or learn.

Decreasing anxiety levels allows an individual to feel more relaxed and calm, thereby reducing hyperactive behaviors like fidgeting or excessive movement.

Individuals with ADHD often experience difficulties sleeping or relaxing, and some traditional medications cause insomnia. With cannabidiol oil, these individuals might find a better sense of energy balance, since one of the effects of the oil is to calm and relax a person.

The balance that CBD can bring the human body might help with other symptoms of ADHD, such as disorganization and scattered thoughts. Though research is still in its early phases, it shows significant promise.

How CBD oil works to help with ADHD symptoms

As previously discussed, cannabidiol oil interacts with the body's own endocannabinoid system, specifically the CB1 and CB2 receptors. The endocannabinoid system helps promote and maintain homeostasis within the body and the mind, through both these receptors.

With ADHD, symptoms like hyperactivity and inattention are often the result of an imbalance of energy and stimulants. Since the receptors in the body work to achieve homeostasis, this is where the potential to aid with ADHD symptoms comes in to play.

It's not so much that CBD oil has the potential to combat or actually stop the symptoms associated with ADHD. However, its ability to help the body find and maintain balance within itself are part of a more likely explanation.

Because the information and data is still so new and inconclusive, it's difficult to say or prove the effectiveness of CBD oil in treating the symptoms of ADHD.

Most medical professionals are likely going to recommend that individuals refrain from switching their medications for CBD oil, especially in more severe cases.

However, there are doctors across the country who have in fact begun recommending CBD oil as a method of treatment to their patients, so it's not an unheard of practice.

Can you use CBD oil on children with ADHD?

First and foremost, it is always essential that any parents considering alternative methods of treatment for their children should always consult with their child's doctor or pediatrician.

Studies show that there are significant neurological and cognitive delays in individuals who use cannabis prior to the age of sixteen. Before this, children are still growing, and the brain is still developing. Subjecting the brain to cannabis before it is significantly and fully developed can be detrimental in the long run.

It is again important to distinguish between marijuana products and CBD products. Marijuana contains THC, the main psychoactive compound in marijuana, while CBD contains no mind-altering substances. It's also important to point out that studies examining the effects of long term CBD use on children are in their early stages, and so there is not yet a definitive answer on questions about the long term impact.

In another sense, legally, yes, parents can give CBD to their children. It is likely their pediatrician or doctor will recommend sticking to the more traditional and proven methods of treatment regarding ADHD. Many experts believe there is still much to learn about ADHD and CBD oil.

Much of today's conversation around CBD oil and its usage, comes from the originally controversial case of Charlotte Figi, a young girl who was born with a very severe case of childhood epilepsy.

Her symptoms were so severe, that at just a few years of age, she was unable to talk or eat and was wheel-chair bound. At the pinnacle of her illness, she was having 300 seizures a week, with many failed treatment attempts behind her.

Desperate, her parents found out about a CBD strain created by Stanley Brothers out of Colorado, with an extremely high CBD content and remarkably low THC content.

Soon after beginning her on a regimen of this oil, Charlotte had no seizures and her cognitive and neurological growth moved forward. The quality of life for her had significantly improved, with no apparent negative side effects.

FDA approved Epidiolex, the only CBD product available by prescription, to treat severe cases of childhood epilepsy. This product significantly boosted the idea of CBD oil being considered a safe method of treatment for children in the right cases.

Though studies have only just begun, CBD as a compound has been around since the early 1900's. It has been tested and explored since scientists first discovered the ability to separate CBD and THC from one another in their corresponding hemp varietals.

Research of CBDs effects is still in the early stages for both adults and children. While most of the research clearly supports the impact of CBD on anxiety, stress, and epilepsy, the research is still very raw on connections with ADHD.

Side effects potentially include: weight loss, fatigue, nausea, irritability, tiredness, and diarrhea. So experts recommend consulting with a professional before starting any new treatment practice.

For these reasons, if an individual chooses to go forward with their child's treatment, the best method is to start with small doses, and incrementally work up until effects are felt. Be aware of the symptoms and side effects, and closely monitor how the CBD is affecting the child. Always consult with a pediatrician.

CBD popularity at an all-time high among Americans

Although there haven't been many definitive or conclusive studies, some parents have started their children on CBD regimens in place of traditional medicine.

Some parents have found success for their children, especially academically and behaviorally, while on the oil. However, other parents felt that CBD oil had no effect on their child's symptoms, and preferred traditional medicines to treat ADHD. Researchers have also begun looking into the impact of CBD on children with autism, to see if it further lessens symptoms of aggression, hyperactivity, and repetitive behaviors.

Chapter 22: How To Deal With An Adhd Child

By now, you know children with ADHD have a shortage in executive functions such as the ability to organize or complete tasks, and think and plan. It is your duty as a parent to take over and provide extra guidance to your child as he/she slowly acquires executive skills.

By doing this, you can help your child overcome his/her daily challenges as well as divert energy into engaging in positive things. These tiny steps can eventually control and even reduce your child's ADHD symptoms. All of this may sound easy. However, it is not.

Dealing with a child suffering from ADHD can be very frustrating and emotionally draining. Many parents dealing with ADHD afflicted children lose hope and give up, which is very unfortunate.

It is important to understand that an ADHD child does not misbehave, ignore, or embarrass you willingly. He/she also wishes for organization: to make his/her room tidy, sit quietly in class, and do everything you ask him or her to do; however, the child is unsure about how to make this things happen.

When you keep that in mind and react positively towards your child, you can manage your child's ADHD. In addition to that, compassion, patience, and plenty of support will give you an upper hand when dealing with an ADHD child.

Parenting Tips for Parents Dealing With ADHD Children

When dealing with an ADHD child, your input is very important to your child's progress. You have the ability to control many factors that can influence and change your child's disorder symptoms. Below are some tips you as a parent can use to influence your child's fight against ADHD:

Stay calm

Parents should always stay calm. Your child's anger escalates when your goes out of control. When this happens, rest assured the results will be a negative outcome.

Instead of arguing with your child and getting nowhere, try not to engage or diffuse an intense moment. For example, when your child becomes stubborn during homework time, just say "I understand this is not enjoyable for you" follow this up with silence and a loving touch to calm him/her down. When he/she calms down, positively encourage him/he to finish the homework.

Create Structures

Come up with a daily routine for your child and make sure you stick to it every day. Establish habits around homework, meals, playtime, and bedtime. Simple habits like having your child complete his/her homework before supper can provide your child with an essential structure he/she can follow.

Define Rules

Clearly lay down house rules. Make sure your child understands what he/she is supposed to do and at what time. With that said, it is also important to constantly reward good behaviors and punish destructive ones. However, do not be too strict. Keep in mind that children suffering from ADHD are slow in adapting to changes. Allow your child to make mistakes and learn from them. Only punish unhelpful behaviors.

Advocate for Your Child When Suitable

Because of his or her ADHD, you should accommodate your child in certain situations. A good example is letting your child use talking books to learn. However, you should strike a balance between accommodating your child and encouraging him or her to grow his or her abilities. For example, you can let your child use a talking book while at the same time, encouraging him or her to learn how to read by hiring a tutor.

Limit Your Behaviors

You should know that the more you do for your child, the less he/she will do for him/herself. This mostly happens to parents who always feel inclined to rescue their kids. The key should be offering support to your child and not taking the driver's seat. For example, you should only assist your child with homework and not do it for him or her.

Additional Parenting Tips

Give your child space to make his/her on choices

Use reasonable consequences when your child breaks the rules

Avoid muting your strong willed child; instead, mold him/her to use his or her willingness positively.

Break your child's tasks into manageable pieces

Limit your child's distractions such as video games and television.

Encourage your child to exercise

Believe in your child

Dealing With ADHD in School and Education

Parents of ADHD children are very worried about how their children cope with academic functioning. This concern has foundation because ADHD makes it very difficult for children to listen, understand, and focus in class.

So what is the solution to dealing with ADHD in schools?

The key to helping an ADHD student in school is teamwork and communication. It is very important for a parent to collaborate with your child's school faculty to help your child achieve academic success. You should give your child's teachers helpful information such as your child's diagnosis, treatment, how you capture his/her attention and their academic recommendations. All this information will help the teachers set a plan of action that effectively teaches the child what he or she needs to know to achieve educational excellence.

With busy schedules in play, it is almost impossible to frequently scheduled personal meetings with your child's teacher. Below are tactics you can use to keep in touch with your child's teacher:

Use email or mobile phones to communicate

Make a notebook that will be travelling back and forth from you to the teacher through your child.

Give the teacher a couple of stamped self-addresses he or she can use to mail important stuff that cannot be entrusted to your child.

Learn how to reduce the stress that comes with your child's homework. Here are a few tips on how to deal with their homework:

Encourage your child to come up with a strategy that best suits him/her on how to approach his or her homework. Then help him/her make this study strategy a habit.

Remove anything that keeps your child from completing his or her homework.

This could be the TV, game console, toys, or the phone.

Give your child freedom to make his or her own homework decisions like when or how to do it.

If your child is on medication, make sure he or she is on medication during homework and after school activities. This will help the child remain calm.

Help your child discover when he or she can do his/her homework better. Is it immediately after school, before dinner, after a couple of exercises, or while listening to music.

Supporting Your Child

Kids suffering from ADHD do not always respond well to normal parenting techniques. Thus, it is important to educate yourself about ADHD in order to be able to support your child.

Experts recommend parents join parent education and support groups because these groups help parents accept a child's condition, learn essential problem solving skills, and essential how-to-cope with frustrations skills. Through support groups, parents can also learn how to react to their children's disappointing behaviors.

By learning all about ADHD, you become a stronger advocate for your kid.

Chapter 23: Developing A Strategy For Your Child

Up until this point, we've concentrated more on how to identify ADHD in a child and how to identify the problems that are part of the life of the family. By now, you should have a pretty good idea of where your child fits in the whole ADHD picture and you've also come to understand that there are strategies that can be implemented to help your child navigate through life's lessons. You may even be breathing a sigh of relief as you realize that your life doesn't always have to be in such chaos as long as you know what your child can do and how to put it into effect.

There is a lot of truth in the expression, "knowledge is power." It's like any person who is struggling with something that is not readily obvious, once they've received a diagnosis they can relax. A diagnosis, in fact, is a kind of validation, a defense against all those naysayers who want to tell you things like 'it's all in your head,' 'you're a bad parent,' and 'it's not a real problem.' I have seen this happen with hidden physical problems as well. People look perfectly healthy, they don't have a visible limp, they don't show any signs of physical ailments, and so people don't believe they have a real problem. But things change quickly when they have a diagnosis. She has lupus, cancer, heart disease, etc.

It is not that the diagnosis solves the issue, but it validates the patient and those who suffer with them. It gives them something to tell the world so they can start to think of your son or daughter in a different way. With ADHD, this doesn't always happen, but it does help. The family members close to the child now have a framework to work in. Parents can switch from seeing the child as willfully disobedient and stop blaming them for their behavior. Siblings also get to see the child in a whole new light.

While all of that is a relief, it is at this point that the real work begins. You can no longer just go through life 'shooting from the hip' when it comes to your ADHD child. The diagnosis does not change the responsibilities and roles in life that each of you has. A child still has the responsibility of learning life's lessons, and the parents still have the job as primary caretaker, provider, guidance counselor, nurse, chauffeur, and so on. It's time to take this to the next level. It's time to create a plan.

As you come up with a workable plan of action, there are a few basic guidelines that you should keep in mind. By following these, you will be able to help your child get the most out of his or her learning experience. Consider these as the building blocks you will use to develop a strategy for helping your child succeed.

Understand that learning will be different

One of the first things you'll have to grasp is that learning will be different for your ADHD child. While children do pick up core subjects of life through instruction their executive skills they often learned through observation of the people and the environment around them.

No one would question that all children learn differently and at a different pace but with the ADHD child, executive skills are rarely picked up by observation. This child struggles to grasp those concepts that are not obvious and pointed out. That means that you're going to have to make sure that their skills are taught. In this process, you will have to make sure that the child understands what behavior is acceptable, what goals they should try to achieve, and what behavior is not acceptable. Then, you can outline for them a plan of action for each phase of the assignment they need to take and explain each one thoroughly.

These assignments should be done under close supervision at first and then gradually fade out your immediate presence as the child grasps the new principles they are learning.

Stay within the Child's Developmental Level

Many parents have expectations that are far higher than what the child can reasonably achieve. They may expect their five-year-old to be able to do the same things as other children their age but if they have not mastered the executive skills needed to meet those expectations it could place them on a straight path to failure.

Parents must first understand what is normal for children their age and then measure their own child's ability against that. The goal here is to match assignments with the child's ability as a starting point and then help the child build his skills from where he is at, not where you expect him to be.

Start with What is Tangible and Move Towards the Intangible

Whenever we teach life lessons, we start with the tangible. Holding a child's hand as she crosses the street, teaching her how to properly hold an eating utensil, or showing them how to wash dishes will eventually lead to life lessons that teach intangible ideas such as cars can be dangerous, proper etiquette is important, and it is important to be clean.

These are lessons that are essential for every child whether they have ADHD or not, however, in the case of the ADHD child, it is even more important to emphasize the tangible. This will require that you manipulate his tangible environment as a foundation for learning those executive skills he is weak in.

Keep in mind that your presence is also a part of the child's external environment. Becoming a constant reminder of things that need to be done is one way, but there are others. Keeping things in front of them can also serve as a visual reminder of things that need to be done. When it comes to tasks, make sure that the assignments given are short and simple enough that they can complete them within a very short amount of time.

You may also control their environment by limiting the amount of external stimulus to keep them from being drawn into too many distractions. Parties should be small and limit the number of excitable activities they can engage in. If they are very small, hold their hands in crowded places and make sure they understand why you need to.

The general idea is that the child will learn first from the external and over repeated experiences they will eventually internalize the lessons and incorporate them into their daily lives.

Incorporate changes in all areas of the external environment

It is not enough to change one aspect of a child's environment. In order for that child to grasp the lessons given to him, the changes have to include more than their immediate environment. Moving a child into a quieter room with fewer distractions may be a good start, but you need to also consider how you interact with your child and making sure she has appropriate monitoring, interaction with others in the household should also be a part of the environmental changes. Changing the dynamics of the task, the environment, and their interactions simultaneously can make it easier for the child to grasp the fundamentals of whatever lesson you are teaching.

Make Use of the Child's Internal Drive to Help Them Succeed

All children have an internal drive that compels them to learn. A rebellious child, therefore, is not just one that fights his parents but instead is a child that has an internal drive and goal that is different from his parents or other authority figures. This drive is found in all children from babies to teenagers. Learn how to use that drive to motivate your child to learn the lessons you want for him.

This can include a number of rewards for them doing what is expected of them or consequences for going against those expectations. This does not mean giving them a reward for something that should become a part of their everyday life. Rewards can be something as small as praise for a job well done or as grand as a vacation.

To accomplish this, you could give the child a list of options. The primary goal is to get the house clean so options could include washing the dishes, vacuuming the carpet, or dusting the furniture. Notice that there is no outside alternative that does not involve cleaning the house; it does not leave the child with an option outside of the expected behavior. Routines like this on a regular basis will eventually be absorbed into the child's mind as part of a normal routine, and in time he will have less resistance to it. It also helps if the entire family is involved in these types of exercises, so the child does not feel that he is being singled out for this particular lesson.

Once the task is completed satisfactorily, they can have the chosen reward.

Match the Assignment to the Amount of Effort the Child Can Reasonably Expend

There are many types of tasks that children will be expected to do but two types of tasks, in particular, that will require the child to put forth extra effort; those they may not be very good at and those they simply don't like to do. These are the tasks the child is most likely going to be reluctant to do and will put up a measure of resistance when asked.

If it is a task that they struggle to do well, your approach may be to break it down into smaller more easy to handle steps. Break each step down to a size that matches the child's ability to put forth the effort. Do not expect more than that first step from the child. When she masters it make sure you praise her for it. This will give her a sense of accomplishment and satisfaction that will embolden her to be eager to take the next step.

The second type of task you will need to address is the one where the child does not like the job given. This could be something like getting homework done or cleaning up the yard. In many households, this is where the child and the parent butt heads. It becomes a struggle for power and can develop into an ongoing battle that will leave both of you frustrated and disappointed.

Remember, your goal is to get the child to complete the task and override his inner feelings of distaste. Keep in mind, this is a task that the child knows how to do but doesn't like doing it. Try to gauge how difficult the task is to the child and while still requiring them to complete it, modify the task, so it is more palatable. Perhaps getting the child to work for 5 minutes and then taking a break. As they become more willing to tackle the job, you can extend the work time to ten minutes, twenty, thirty or more. Sure, it will take a lot longer to get the job done, but it will get done rather than spending that precious energy in an ongoing battle that may never end.

You might find that at a certain point, the constant stops and starts will be more annoying to the child and they will then finish the task in earnest just so they can get on with something else they would much rather do.

If it is an older child, you can ask him to break down the task into manageable steps so that he feels more empowered. If the steps are done accordingly, and the job gets done both the parents and the child will feel very satisfied and have a sense of accomplishment at the results.

Use Incentives as a Motivator

There is a lot of controversy over whether a child should be given rewards or incentives to do what they should do. I suppose it's that old adage that says a child should do what he is told simply because he is a child. However, that argument is contrary to what a parent's role should be. The parent's primary responsibility is to teach the child how to function in today's world as an adult. Therefore life's lessons should revolve around what they can expect from the world around them.

Rarely do adults do things because it is the right thing to do. They go to work with the expectation of a paycheck, they go to the doctor with an expectation that they will feel better, and they take vacations with the expectation that they will have enjoyment and relaxation. Even God-fearing people pattern their lives by the guidelines that state that they will have an eternal reward at some point in the future. This is the way the world works. So, using incentives to motivate your child to do a certain task fits right in with helping them find their place in the world.

As we pointed out before. This does not mean that an elaborate reward is required for every task. Some children will be motivated enough when they hear a word of praise while others may need a little more incentive to get them to do those harder tasks. By expecting the child to complete the task before the award is given is also a teaching mechanism. It teaches them to delay their gratification, and that working is the only way for them to receive whatever it is they want. No doubt, this is a valuable skill that every child needs to learn regardless of their abilities.

The Support Should Match the Need

This may seem like an obvious one, but it is a little more difficult than you might imagine. Every parent struggles with knowing when to intervene and help their child and when to stand by and let them push ahead on their own. While your heartstrings may pull you to jump in and do something it seems like the child can't do on her own, it is not usually the best course of action.

We've all seen those parents that do their children's homework assignments, hover painfully over their every move and jump in whenever the child begins to falter.

These children rarely progress to the point of independence. They grow up expecting everyone to do things for them and rarely put forth any exertion to accomplish goals themselves. As a parent, you want to manipulate just enough, so the child learns what is expected of him.

For example, a child that is learning how to walk gets up and falls down repeatedly before he learns to balance. A parent may stand over him, holding onto his hands and may nudge him to make a step by pushing his legs against the child's in a walking motion. Eventually, the child will understand what walking is and will tentatively take a few steps on his own. In this way, the child learns to walk. The parents help him to stand by holding him up as he learns how to balance himself. Later, the gentle nudging helps him to understand how to take steps first one leg and then the other.

But what happens if every time the child tries to stand and falls, the parent runs in and swoops him up in their arms and comforts him? That parent has interrupted the learning process. Parents should be close in case the child needs assistance but far enough away that he can make a move on his own. Ideally, parents should be there as an observer until the child reaches a point where he can no longer move forward in a task, and then demonstrate the next step in a way that the child will understand.

Keep Support in Place Until it is No Longer Needed

Remember, dealing with ADHD is not about the child understanding a specific task but is about them sustaining the mindset to do that task. This is an easy concept to understand in words but not so easy to remember in a given situation. For example, a child that is learning how to organize his room will understand the idea that books go on the shelves, toys go in the toy box, and clothing goes in the closet. Many parents may walk a child through this process several times, and once they see that the child fully grasps the concept and the importance of it, they remove their presence and expect the child to function independently from then on.

The problem with this is that the child has only grasped the fundamentals of what is expected but not yet learned it as a life habit. As soon as the parent pulls out of the picture, distractions can and will come in, and he will lose interest in the task. Ideally, parents will keep their support and presence with the child until they are sure that he has mastered the task and has made it a part of his regular routine.

Changes in Supervision Should be Done Gradually

Finally, when you do withdraw support, it should be done so gradually. As the child learns to perform each phase of a task independently, allow them that independence but remain close by in case, they need additional support. Many parents focus on an all or nothing approach which leaves the child floundering when a constant presence is no longer there. Once the child learns a specific task, step away for a moment or two and then gradually increase that time away until he is completely independent.

Of course, the preceding list of guidelines to use in preparing a working strategy for teaching your child is not a fool-proof system. Every parent will have to adjust their methods accordingly to fit the needs of their child. However, from understanding these basic concepts and how to work with an ADHD child, parents will be more relaxed having a basic understanding of how these affect the child and the benefits that can be gained.

Chapter 24: Attention Deficit Disorder Diet

While there are many reasons for ADD and ADHD, one of them that is both important and relatively easy to control is a modified attention deficit disorder diet.

Simply by removing certain foods from the diet, you can greatly reduce, if not completely eliminate, your child's ADHD. A diet for attention deficit disorder may indeed take care of the problem altogether, although oftentimes, what happens is that symptoms are simply eased to the point of manageability.

Here are some things you should remove from your child's diet, no questions asked. You should try removal of these items for at least two weeks before you decide the removal has no effect.

Sugar And Most Caffeine

Children with ADD already have difficulty controlling impulses. The inclusion of a lot of sugar or any caffeine in the diet can just make the symptoms worse. Therefore, removing these substances eliminates potential triggers for ADD symptoms. If you can't go to absolutely zero sugar, cut it to just 10% of its previous levels.

Dairy Products

Oftentimes, children's ADD symptoms can be made worse or even manifest if they're allergic to something. Dairy products are among the most common of allergens for children. Therefore, eliminate all dairy products, especially milk. If you need a milk substitute, try rice or almond milk, or a product called Better Than Milk.

Have your child drink a lot of water and eliminate other beverages that might also cause problems, like tea (because of the caffeine), soda (because of artificial colors, sugars, flavouring and caffeine), or sports drinks such as Gatorade. Try just water for two weeks. Your child will complain for a few days, but very soon will get used to the taste. It's a good idea to buy a water filter if you use tap water so as to remove any unpleasant taste and odors. Again, this is healthier, and will also eliminate chemicals that are unhealthy. See? There is a plus side for an attention deficit disorder diet.

Junk food

No processed salty, sugary, white flour foods. If it's junk (meaning empty calories), your child can't eat it. (That includes some breakfast cereals, by the way.)

Fruit Juice

This might surprise you, but juice has a lot of sugar content, which can exacerbate your child's ADD symptoms. If you must, dilute the fruit juice with water to at most 50% strength, less than that if you can.

Chocolate

A tiny amount is okay very occasionally, but no more than a tiny piece once a week.

NutraSweet or other artificial sweeteners

Absolutely no artificial sweeteners.

Processed meats or MSG

Avoid processed meats or foods with MSG in them.

Fried foods

At most, your child can have 10% of the previous amount eaten.

Food Coloring

Many children are sensitive to food coloring used in food substances like Kool-Aid. Eliminate these for two weeks completely. Now, you might think that this attention deficit disorder diet is very restrictive, and it is, based upon modern standards. However, good, simple, natural foods are available. They just require some cooking.

Get yourself some recipe books or go on the Internet to search for recipes that use only whole ingredients with nothing added. Things like meat, potatoes, fresh and frozen vegetables with no salt, sugar artificially ingredients added, and so on.

After the elimination period, you can begin to add some of these listed foods back, slowly. Keep in mind, though, that these are not healthy foods for the most part, anyway, so you may want to just eliminate them permanently from your child's diet and from the rest of your family's, too.

Once you begin to add these foods back in (especially things like dairy, which can be quite healthful and which you may want to keep in your diet), watch your child for reactions. Usually, you should see this type of reaction within four days of the foods' ingestion. You may see physical subtle signs like red blotches or red ears, or behavioral changes like explosive temper tantrums. After about a month, you should know what foods to avoid.

Feeding Your Child's Brain

A healthy brain needs healthy foods. Breakfast is best done as a high-protein, low carbohydrate meal. Shoot for 60% protein and 40% carbohydrates for this meal and choose things like eggs. If your child doesn't like eggs, you can use protein supplements like shakes to help your child get extra protein. There are many "just protein" shakes on the market that has no artificial colors, flavors, or sugar. They can be quite bland, so you can be creative and make shakes from rice milk, a banana, some protein powder and a little carob powder if you wish.

A good quality multivitamin and mineral supplement made for children

Remember to buy one that has no artificial colors and flavors added.

Fish Oil

These come as capsules so your child doesn't have to taste the "fish" taste if he or she doesn't like the flavor. Fish oil feeds the brain with omega-3 fatty acids for proper food. Most children need between one and two capsules a day.

(Avoid these capsules if your child has any type of blood coagulation problem or other condition that may result in blood thinning. It's a good idea to check with your doctor, too.)

Fruits and vegetables

Go organic if at all possible. This helps ensure that your child has no pesticides in his or her diet, either.

You should see improvement in as little as two weeks to a month. Again, the diet for attention deficit disorder may not completely eradicate behavioural symptoms, but most likely, they'll certainly lessen. An attention deficit disorder diet will be much more effective when combined with other natural ADHD alternative treatments, such as homoeopathic remedies.

Chapter 25: Try Making Simple Changes In Your Diet

Some will claim that there is a lack of solid research that supports the claim that some dietary changes can have a positive impact on lessening the symptoms of ADHD. However, many parents who have taken such a step of making changes to the daily diet of their children will tell you that it is worth doing.

By introducing a diet that is balanced and healthy, the ADHD symptoms have been easier to manage. And one thing is clear that poor nutrition can have a negative effect on just about anyone, no matter if they have ADHD or not.

Start By Cutting Back On Sugar!

Those with ADHD will see the benefits when they cut back on sugar in their diet. Sugar is a trigger for hyper activity, especially in children. Those who have been diagnosed with ADHD and have a high sugar intake within their daily diet will usually have trouble with their blood sugar levels. These fluctuations in the level of blood sugar results in mood swings and bouts of irritability.

Kids with ADHD that fall into this category will also tend to have bouts of mood swings, aggressive behavior and hyperactivity. So as you can see, sugar intake needs to be reduced to help lessen or avoid these symptoms.

Reducing The Amount Of Refined Carbohydrate

Research has shown that a diet high in protein and low in carbohydrates can reduce the symptoms of ADHD. But it is advised that the carbohydrates are not cut out completely. It is just a case of reducing those foods that have a high level of carbohydrates.

Foods to cut back on include white flour and white sugar as well as processed foods that contain additives, artificial colors and flavorings.

Refined carbohydrates do have a bad effect on blood sugar levels. Too much refined carbs in the body will make the symptoms worse.

If carbohydrates are to be consumed, these should be in the form of complex carbohydrates. This type of carbohydrates are unrefined. The types of food which are considered as complex carbohydrates include all types of fruit, whole grains and vegetables.

Know The Trigger Foods And Avoid Them As Much As You Can

ADHD symptoms can be aggravated by various foods. As an example, it has been shown that food containing additives such as colorings, artificial flavorings, sweeteners and preservatives can trigger problems in behavior.

Those with ADHD should steer clear of these types of processed foods. If in doubt, always read the food ingredients label on the packaging.

It is also worth mentioning that some people with ADHD also have their symptoms triggered by wheat, eggs, dairy products and orange juice.

As mentioned earlier, a diet that is great for ADHD should be based on wholesome and natural foods. It may involve some testing to see what works and what doesn't but it will be worth the effort. Once you get it right, a great improvement can be seen and the symptoms will become more manageable.

Conclusion

ADHD is something a person can not choose to take off like a jacket. It is a disorder that can make or break a person and those around them.

There are those that ADHD is imaginary and all in the mind. These are people who should not be listened to. If you have to live with it, then you know it's real, no matter what that so called 'expert' thinks!

I hope that this publication has given you some advice, ideas and suggestions that you find useful to help you on your journey of living with ADHD.

What seems like a disadvantage to others could be used as an advantage by you. All you need to do is make things work for you, seek as much advice as you can and never stop asking questions.

I wish you all the best!

www.ingramcontent.com/pod-product-compliance
Lightning Source LLC
Chambersburg PA
CBHW051723020426
42333CB00014B/1121